ABOUT THE AUTHOR

Manny Aston began his creative journey in film and television before making his mark as a playwright. His play *Fossils!* has been performed internationally and by countless schools across Australia. He is also the author of *Study Right*, a best-selling study skills guide with over 20,000 copies sold. With a career in education spanning more than 35 years, Manny has served as a senior lecturer, professor, and academic dean. He holds bachelor's, master's, and doctoral degrees in psychology, education, mass communication, philosophy, and the creative arts. Based in Sydney with his family, Manny has restored an old pinball machine, plays the trumpet quite badly, and owns way too many typewriters.

ALSO BY MANNY ASTON

Plays
Fossils!
When the Bough Breaks
Clay Soldiers

Study skills
Study Right: A simple guide to successful study
Study Smart: A guide to successful study at TAFE

HOW TO BE
A ROTTEN STUDENT:
A PERSONAL MANIFESTO

DR MANNY ASTON

REEDY
BOOKS

How to be a Rotten Student
© Manny Aston, 2025

All rights reserved. No part of this publication may be reproduced, stored in a retrieval system, or transmitted in any form or by any means—electronic, mechanical, photocopying, recording, or otherwise—without the prior written permission of the copyright owner, except for brief quotations used in reviews or scholarly works.

First published in 2025
by Reedy Books, Sydney
www.reedybooks.com.au

ISBN: 978-1-7641262-0-5

Cover design: Jason Gemenis
Typeset in: Garamond 12 point
Printed and bound in Australia

The information contained in this book is for general informational purposes only. While the author and publisher have made every effort to ensure that the information in this book is accurate at the time of publication, they assume no responsibility for errors, omissions, or contrary interpretation of the subject matter herein.

 A catalogue record for this book is available from the National Library of Australia

Author Contact: mannyaston.com

10 9 8 7 6 5 4 3 2 1

HOW TO BE A ROTTEN STUDENT: A PERSONAL MANIFESTO

DR MANNY ASTON

REEDY BOOKS

How to be a Rotten Student
© Manny Aston, 2025

All rights reserved. No part of this publication may be reproduced, stored in a retrieval system, or transmitted in any form or by any means—electronic, mechanical, photocopying, recording, or otherwise—without the prior written permission of the copyright owner, except for brief quotations used in reviews or scholarly works.

First published in 2025
by Reedy Books, Sydney
www.reedybooks.com.au

ISBN: 978-1-7641262-0-5

Cover design: Jason Gemenis
Typeset in: Garamond 12 point
Printed and bound in Australia

The information contained in this book is for general informational purposes only. While the author and publisher have made every effort to ensure that the information in this book is accurate at the time of publication, they assume no responsibility for errors, omissions, or contrary interpretation of the subject matter herein.

 A catalogue record for this book is available from the National Library of Australia

Author Contact: mannyaston.com

10 9 8 7 6 5 4 3 2 1

*This book is dedicated with love to my family:
Oma, Leanne, Christopher, Gabriella, Emily
and now Laurence.
These are the people who make my life such an absolute joy.
My dad's not around anymore, but in my heart, he still is.*

CONTENTS

1. A ROTTEN CHAPTER 1 .... *1*
  • Who reads a preface anyway? • The world according to Peanuts • Ferris Bueller's Day Off • The long and winding road • A personal manifesto

2. WHAT STRESS ISN'T *12*
  • Pressure is a privilege • An uncomfortable paradox • Snowballs and boiling frogs • The perfect storm • The human cost of academic anxiety

3. PSYCHOBABBLE *27*
  • Defusing a bomb • Deconstructing Josh • Cognitive restructuring • Hope for the best • Food for thought

4. THE EDUCATION SYSTEM *44*
  • Prison and preschool • Freshman and sophomores • The business of education • Publish or perish • Algebra in the coffee lounge

5. KNOWLEDGE & LEARNING *59*
  • The illusion of knowing • Learners inherit the earth • Why my dog will never get his PhD • Bobo and beyond • Humuhumunukunukuapua'a

6. INFORMATION OVERLOAD *71*
  • Defining existence • The 5000 ton book • Why I love Wikipedia • Choice, complexity, chaos • HAL 9000

7. THE STUDENT MINDSET..*87*
- Welcome to the Frisbee club • Failing the fun run • How to become a zombie • Don't be scared of change • My Pulitzer Prize

8. DO LESS … SIMPLIFY *99*
- Less is more • Don't read your textbook • A guide to cramming • The myth of 'multitasking' • The KISS principle

9. PROCRASTINATION *113*
- Macbeth, Act V, Scene V • Pressure creates diamonds • Smoke and mirrors • Task decomposition • Embrace the deadline

10. THE MAGIC OF 50% *126*
- Stephen Hawking got it wrong • Goldilocks got it right • When good enough is not good enough • The beauty of half-way • All work and no play

11. THE ART OF FAILING *139*
- Self-consciously rusticated • What a cactus and trampoline have in common • Nothing is impossible … almost • Turn on, tune in, drop out • The Concorde Fallacy

12. A ROTTEN FINAL CHAPTER *155*
- What am I doing right? • Formalised curiosity • No need to grow up dude • My Alien • Finding your 'place'

ACKNOWLEDGEMENTS..*168*

REFERENCES *170*

THE ROTTEN STUDENT MANIFESTO..............................*179*

1. A ROTTEN CHAPTER 1

There's no heavier burden than great potential.

Linus
You're a Brave Man, Charlie Brown

Who reads a preface anyway?

The preface of a book will usually have a rationale as to why it was written, give an insight into the way it was developed and broadly give you an idea of what areas it will cover. You usually find it *before* Chapter 1. But, let's face it; who reads the preface of a book ... nobody, right? Except maybe, people who want to see if their name is in it somewhere. So here I am disguising my preface as Chapter 1 to a) encourage you to actually read it; and b) give the book an extra chapter. Without it, I would only have 11 chapters, and I don't know about you, but to me that is an uncomfortable number; 12 is far more symmetrical.

I started this book with two questions in mind: what things about study should students know; and what do I wish someone would have told me when I was a student. The 'what should you know' category is pretty broad. If we're looking at study-related stress, it certainly helps to know a little bit about stress itself, and perhaps have a few strategies in place to deal with it. As a student, you are part of the education system which in turn is a part of the world of knowledge and learning – there are chapters on each of these areas. We are all dependent on the ever-evolving minefield of information that is out there, along with the technology that goes with it. I thought it was important to write about that as well.

When it comes to the 'things I wish someone would have told me' it gets a little more complicated. There is a lot of good advice floating around – books, apps, websites, workshops, you name it. So my approach is unashamedly personal. What would I do if I were about to embark on a course of study right now. Preparing yourself and developing a good mindset is critical, as is keeping things simple. Dealing with procrastination is one of the biggest issues students face, along with perfectionism. While there are hundreds of books on success, there are not too many that deal with failure. Failure for some students signifies the end of their studies, when it may well be a beginning. Finally, I

1. A ROTTEN CHAPTER 1

There's no heavier burden than great potential.

Linus
You're a Brave Man, Charlie Brown

Who reads a preface anyway?

The preface of a book will usually have a rationale as to why it was written, give an insight into the way it was developed and broadly give you an idea of what areas it will cover. You usually find it *before* Chapter 1. But, let's face it; who reads the preface of a book … nobody, right? Except maybe, people who want to see if their name is in it somewhere. So here I am disguising my preface as Chapter 1 to a) encourage you to actually read it; and b) give the book an extra chapter. Without it, I would only have 11 chapters, and I don't know about you, but to me that is an uncomfortable number; 12 is far more symmetrical.

I started this book with two questions in mind: what things about study should students know; and what do I wish someone would have told me when I was a student. The 'what should you know' category is pretty broad. If we're looking at study-related stress, it certainly helps to know a little bit about stress itself, and perhaps have a few strategies in place to deal with it. As a student, you are part of the education system which in turn is a part of the world of knowledge and learning – there are chapters on each of these areas. We are all dependent on the ever-evolving minefield of information that is out there, along with the technology that goes with it. I thought it was important to write about that as well.

When it comes to the 'things I wish someone would have told me' it gets a little more complicated. There is a lot of good advice floating around – books, apps, websites, workshops, you name it. So my approach is unashamedly personal. What would I do if I were about to embark on a course of study right now. Preparing yourself and developing a good mindset is critical, as is keeping things simple. Dealing with procrastination is one of the biggest issues students face, along with perfectionism. While there are hundreds of books on success, there are not too many that deal with failure. Failure for some students signifies the end of their studies, when it may well be a beginning. Finally, I wanted to share some of the lessons I've learned in my 35 years as a teacher (and almost as long as a student).

Study-related stress isn't just an isolated thing; it's contextual. It's dependent on a range of other factors: the subject you are studying, where you are studying, your teacher, your family, fellow-students, or your work, to name but a few. So, this is not a 'how to study' book; it's a 'how to *live with* study' book. It's about being a better student by seemingly being a rotten student. I've used the word 'seemingly' because being better by being worse is somewhat of a contradiction. While this book is aimed at all students, it will be particularly useful to those who find study stressful or overwhelming.

The world according to Peanuts

As a child, discovering my first *Peanuts* paperback in a small second-hand bookstore was a near religious experience. I related to almost all of the characters. There was Charlie Brown, the all-round-good guy, hoping for the best, but often expecting the worst (that's me). Linus is the philosopher of the group, never separated from his blue security blanket (I actually had a blue security blanket). There's Pig-Pen, who finds it impossible to stay clean and walks around surrounded by his own personal cloud of dust (no comment). And of course, we can't forget the much loved beagle,

Snoopy in the guise of his alter-egos "Joe Cool" or "World Famous Author."

A memorable sequence from one of my early bookshop finds, *You're a Brave Man, Charlie Brown*, is very relevant when considering the themes of this book; "I'm doomed! I didn't make the Honour Roll this month," Linus confides to Charlie Brown. This will be a great disappointment to Linus' parents who want him to be "the smartest kid in the world." He arrives home, yelling "I'm home. I'm home from school" (in bold and all-caps), then in very small font, "I didn't make the Honour Roll." This exchange became a running joke between my father and me, whenever I didn't do as well as expected in my studies – even when I was at university.

Education is a big deal in many cultures, including the European one. My family background is Hungarian, and in our household going to university was expected; getting a degree represented learning, achievement and status. When I obtained my doctorate my great aunt (who was 101 when she died) proudly announced to everybody, "We have another doctor in the family," (her husband was a prominent Sydney psychiatrist in the 1960s). "I'm not that kind of doctor, Aunty ... I'm an *academic* doctor." She looked at me sternly, "It doesn't matter ... a doctor is a doctor." This was the environment I grew up in. My cousins Peter and Nick, were constantly told they should be, "more like Manny."

The fallout of Linus not making the Honour Roll was generalised disappointment, "My mother's upset, my father's upset, my teacher's upset, the principal's upset … good grief!" However, it's the final line that carries the most resonance, when Linus laments, "There's no heavier burden than great potential!" I was that kid with 'potential'. Arriving to a new country for my first years of formal education without speaking a word of English certainly made for a fairly slow start. It took close to 10 years for me to really catch up, and probably another 25 years to feel even remotely confident as a student. In my eyes, I was at heart a rotten student, except most people hadn't quite figured that out yet.

Ferris Bueller's Day Off

When I was younger I would occasionally take a 'day off' school ("wagging" is the colloquial term; truancy is a little more harsh). My parents both worked full-time so I would have the house to myself. I'd head to the local shop, buy some chocolate, and spend a relaxed day eating, reading and watching television. My parents would arrive home, find me diligently doing my homework and be none the wiser. Happy days.

This little escapade reminds me of one of my favourite movies, *Ferris Bueller's Day Off.* It's a classic

John Hughes comedy about a high school senior who fakes being sick to skip school and have a fun day with his friends, all while trying to outsmart his suspicious principal. But more than just being really funny, the film reminds us to live in the moment, take time to enjoy life, and not let fear or strict rules stop us from having a bit of fun.

Fun is not usually a word people associate with study, but there is no real reason for that to be the case. You can study for an exam, but you can also study a recipe, a piece of music or the instructions for building Lego; it's not necessarily meant to be serious. There are plenty of other things in this world that *are* serious, but study doesn't have to be one of them. Learning and knowledge is a wonderful thing, but unfortunately for many students it's far from wonderful.

A quick Google search on study-related stress is quite an eye-opener. Surveys show a large number of students registering anxiety symptoms high enough to be of clinical concern; in fact, a majority of students found their entire academic experience to be stressful. It's no surprise; the pressure to achieve starts early. I recently saw an advert for pre-kindergarten tuition!

The fact that study can cause stress and unhappiness for so many people has never sat well with me. It is one of the main reasons I have written this book; study is a pathway to learning, and learning should be a relatively enjoyable process. For me, an occasional dose of television and chocolate definitely made my life as a student better. That's the aim of this book - making your life as a student more enjoyable and less stressful. As Ferris Bueller says, "Life moves pretty fast. If you don't stop and look around once in a while, you could miss it.'"

The long and winding road

I've always found the process of writing quite torturous. I am literally wracking my brain trying to recall if I have *ever* really enjoyed writing anything. Make no mistake; I enjoy *the result* of writing, but not necessarily the process itself. I'm certainly not alone; plenty of famous (and not so famous) writers didn't really enjoy the process. When faced with a writing task, weeding the garden seems like an excellent alternative, as does cataloguing my library, sorting nuts and bolts in my workshop, or even writing anything *other* than what I'm supposed to. Weeks would pass without any progress. I would make elaborate plans on spreadsheets, only to fall behind on the first day.

It dawned on me that most of the things that have happened to me while writing this book will most probably happen to you while studying. I procrastinated, rewrote, doubted myself, doubted the whole book – wondered why I'm writing it in the first place. Then in a blinding flash of inspiration I would find some sort of path through the clutter, rewrite everything, only to find that the first version was probably better. This book has been re-written more than any other piece of work I've ever completed. The version you are now reading is virtually a completely different book than the one I started with.

But rest assured every single emotion I experienced while writing this book is closely replicated by the emotions and experiences of millions of students around the world every hour of every day. Students have high expectations, they often feel immense pressure to achieve top grades and meet family or societal expectations.

The sheer volume of material to learn can feel overwhelming, especially with tight deadlines and frequent assessments. It can be difficult to set aside time to get work done. It's often a struggle to get started, and then even more of a struggle to finish. You try and do too much without proper rest; you get exhausted, stressed, and less motivated. It's easy to lose focus and direction. Your self-confidence is severely tested. But trust me, there are strategies to deal with all of this.

Writing and studying are both journeys of discovery. Both require patience, revision, and a willingness to deal with uncertainty. Progress is often invisible until suddenly it just clicks. It's very rare to produce a flawless enjoyable process. For me, an occasional dose of television and chocolate definitely made my life as a student better. That's the aim of this book - making your life as a student more enjoyable and less stressful. As Ferris Bueller says, "Life moves pretty fast. If you don't stop and look around once in a while, you could miss it.'"

The long and winding road

I've always found the process of writing quite torturous. I am literally wracking my brain trying to recall if I have *ever* really enjoyed writing anything. Make no mistake; I enjoy *the result* of writing, but not necessarily the process itself. I'm certainly not alone; plenty of famous (and not so famous) writers didn't really enjoy the process. When faced with a writing task, weeding the garden seems like an excellent alternative, as does cataloguing my library, sorting nuts and bolts in my workshop, or even writing anything *other* than what I'm supposed to. Weeks would pass without any progress. I would make elaborate plans on spreadsheets, only to fall behind on the first day.

It dawned on me that most of the things that have happened to me while writing this book will most probably happen to you while studying. I procrastinated, rewrote, doubted myself, doubted the whole book – wondered why I'm writing it in the first place. Then in a blinding flash of inspiration I would find some sort of path through the clutter, rewrite everything, only to find that the first version was probably better. This book has been re-written more than any other piece of work I've ever completed. The version you are now reading is virtually a completely different book than the one I started with.

But rest assured every single emotion I experienced while writing this book is closely replicated by the emotions and experiences of millions of students around the world every hour of every day. Students have high expectations, they often feel immense pressure to achieve top grades and meet family or societal expectations.

The sheer volume of material to learn can feel overwhelming, especially with tight deadlines and frequent assessments. It can be difficult to set aside time to get work done. It's often a struggle to get started, and then even more of a struggle to finish. You try and do too much without proper rest; you get exhausted, stressed, and less motivated. It's easy to lose focus and direction. Your self-confidence is severely tested. But trust me, there are strategies to deal with all of this.

Writing and studying are both journeys of discovery. Both require patience, revision, and a willingness to deal with uncertainty. Progress is often invisible until suddenly it just clicks. It's very rare to produce a flawless first draft; there is no instant mastery. Writers return to their words again and again, refining meaning and structure, just like students revisit ideas to deepen their understanding. To quote The Beatles, it's a "long and winding road."

There will be moments of inspiration and clarity, but also times when progress feels slow or uncertain. What matters is sticking with it. It's often the unexpected twists, the mistakes, and the countless revisions that lead to real insight and growth. These detours aren't distractions ... they're part of the journey. In the end, it's not just about arriving at a destination, but about who you become along the way.

A personal manifesto

I love the word 'manifesto'. It doesn't muck around, it means business. It's a public declaration of a person or group's principles and goals. It aims to inspire action, provoke thought, or establish a shared vision. They're usually politically motivated (think Karl Marx), but can be cultural, social or even corporate. The art world is definitely big on manifestos (most of the major modern art movements had them), but really ... anyone can write one.

What makes a manifesto a little different from a simple statement is that there is usually some sort of call to reform. When statistics reflect the number of students who are miserable – there *should* be some sort of reform. This book is intended to help students put their studies in perspective. It's a *personal* manifesto, because it's what I think – for better or for worse. It consists of opinions and advice that I want to share with you as if you were sitting with me over a cup of coffee or in one of my classes. That objective has defined the style and tone of this book.

You'll notice that I use parentheses a lot (like this). Most style guides advocate using them sparingly and purposefully as they're generally not considered to be good writing style. I like them. It gives me a chance to throw in an extra little comment here and there.

Each chapter of this book is divided into five bite-sized chunks. This structure was adopted during the drafting process and ultimately I saw no need to change it – the symmetry and consistency appealed to me. It was simply a way of organising my thoughts during the early stages of writing, without writing too much or writing too little. As the book developed my goal was to make each sub-section self contained, easy to read and interesting, relating something of my own experiences whenever I could. My aim was for each section to make a point and give some practical advice the reader could "put in their pocket" and take away with them – a "pocket-point," as it were. Some points have made their way into the Rotten Student Manifesto, which is included at the end of this book.

I've grown up surrounded by quotes. My mother would bring me ones she found on her desk diary. My father used to hand write them, or cut them out (tear out, really) from whatever he was reading. I'd go out to my office and find he'd pinned a new one to the noticeboard on the wall in front of my desk, which is where many of them still remain. It should be no surprise that I've not only chosen to start each chapter with a quote, but have used them liberally throughout the book (in some instances straight from the noticeboard).

I've thought a lot about the chapters that you are about to read. You can never get it 100% right, and you can't please everyone, but I'm very happy with what I've written. I genuinely hope you enjoy it.

2. WHAT STRESS ISN'T

Stress ... in addition to being itself and
the result of itself, is also the cause of itself.

Ffrangcon Roberts
Medical educator and researcher

Pressure is a privilege

Every tennis player who heads out on to centre court of the Arthur Ashe Stadium, will walk past a plaque with the words "Pressure is a privilege," proudly displayed. It's a timely reminder of the honour that comes with competing at the highest levels of sport. The quote, by American tennis legend Billie Jean King, presents pressure as a positive force, something to be accepted as a pathway to success.

It's a good way to look at it, as originally the word 'stress' referred to physical tightness or pressure. In the 17th century, the word began to appear in physics and engineering; it described the internal force exerted within materials when subjected to pressure, ultimately resulting in it breaking. We still associate stress with being 'under pressure' or reaching 'breaking point'.

The gradual evolution of the word into the world of human experience can be attributed mainly to the work of Walter Cannon. Cannon was a medical doctor whose seminal work, *The wisdom of the body*, introduced the concept of the "fight or flight" response, describing how animals (including humans) respond to threats by either confronting them or fleeing from them. So in that context, the impact of stress was considered neutral if not positive; it was what enabled an organism to survive.

Billie Jean King wanted to say something encouraging to motivate her team-mate, Lindsay Davenport, before the 1998 US Open final. That's when she said, "pressure is a privilege, and champions adjust." Davenport won in straight sets to claim her first Grand Slam singles title. It's the first part of the quote that is generally used; the second part is often left out, perhaps because not everyone 'adjusts'. For many people, pressure and stress can have negative psychological and emotional consequences.

In the 1930s, Hans Selye explored the body's biological responses to challenging or threatening situations. He observed that stress, which he likened to wear and tear on the body, triggered a series of physical responses. Selye published his findings in numerous works, the most notable being his 1956 book, *The stress of life*. It was an important work as it popularised the concept of stress and provided a framework for understanding how chronic stress could contribute to disease and an overall decline in health.

Today, the word 'stress' describes anything from the pressure of assessment deadlines to personal life challenges. The notion of stress is now more often related to the fast pace of life rather than immediate survival. Stress and pressure are hard to avoid in a modern world as it's a natural part of being human. The advent of technology, 24/7 connectivity, and social media has led to a unique type of stress, one that our ancestors didn't have to contend with.

Students are magnets for stress. The process of study brings with it assessment deadlines, presentations, and exams. With the end of semester looming, it's not at all unusual to find my daughter Emily wandering around the house chanting her now familiar mantra, "I'm stressed; I'm stressed," and eventually curling up into a foetal position on the floor. I somehow don't think she would appreciate it if I took the opportunity to remind her that "pressure is a privilege."

An uncomfortable paradox

Stress is one of a unique set of conditions that can be both the symptom and the illness all at the same time. I love the quote by noted medical educator and researcher, Ffrangcon Roberts: stress, "in addition to being itself and the result of itself, is also the cause of itself." While this might initially seem, in the words of Dr Roberts an "uncomfortable paradox," it is worth unpacking the three main elements buried within the statement. We have a person's perception of stress ("being itself"), the psychological or physical response to the stress ("the result of itself") and a 'stressor' ("the cause of itself)."

The term stressor is quite common in the world of psychology; essentially referring to any external pressures or challenges, specific events, situations or even people. An assessment deadline or upcoming exam would be a good example. Virtually anything can be a stressor; as our quote indicates, even stress itself. Typically, we respond to stressors by exhibiting some sort of physical, emotional, or behavioural reaction. Some people may experience an increased heart rate and elevated blood pressure (remember, 'fight or flight'), while others become more irritable, lose sleep, or find it difficult to concentrate. The list of symptoms is almost endless.

Pinpointing precisely what qualifies as being a stressor is tricky because quite a bit hinges on whether *we perceive* something as stressful or not. If we don't perceive a situation or event as stressful, then there is no stressor involved. For example, I genuinely don't find exams stressful. They can be tedious, or an imposition, but mainly because I have to spend time studying for them. My wife on the other hand finds them stressful. If we both sat the same exam, for her it would be a stressor. And even then, it's still not 100 percent black and white. Does she find *all* exams stressful or only ones she hasn't prepared well enough for? So after a little detective-work, the stressor may not be exams as such, but the 'lack of preparation'.

#1. It's only stress if you perceive it to be.

Needless to say, stress is a big topic with a lot written about it, both current and historic. There is also a great deal of confusion, misinformation and money involved. Make no mistake; the stress industry is big business. There are tablets designed to reduce it, courses developed to avoid it and entire professions devoted to treat it. The interesting thing is that many people treat stress in the same way they would treat an illness ... which it isn't.

Stress itself is not an illness, but it can *cause* illness. It is a physical, emotional and behavioural response to internal or external factors that impact on our lives. An 'internal' factor is something that is self-imposed such as, negative thinking, perfectionism, or poor self esteem. External factors can include assessment deadlines, financial pressures, relationship conflicts, or major life changes. The consequences of stress can be both positive and negative. So, stress can motivate you to focus, meet deadlines, or prepare for an important exam. But the negative effects of stress can lead to anxiety, burnout, or health issues when it persists without proper management.

Snowballs and boiling frogs

I was born in Hamburg which is in the northern part of Germany. Some of my earliest memories involve throwing snowballs. However, I don't think I ever rolled a snowball down a hill to see if it would get bigger; like they do in the cartoons.

A small snowball starts at the top of a hill, rolls down, and gathers more and more snow until it becomes an enormous, unstoppable ball (often with our unfortunate animated friend trapped inside). As you've probably guessed I'm using the snowball as a metaphor to describe any situation where a small action or event builds up on itself leading to something much bigger. The insidious thing about stress is that it can build on itself and spiral out of control without you noticing.

In real life, snowballs can roll down hills and get bigger, but it's rare. The whole process depends on a fairly specific set of conditions. The snow needs to be 'sticky', the hill needs to have a steady slope, and the snowball can't be too small. Lack of sleep, poor nutrition, and lack of exercise are perfect conditions for stress to start rolling down the hill. All three affect cognitive function, memory, and mood, which impacts academic performance and mental health (snowball forming), which leads to increased anxiety (getting bigger) which leads to less sleep, even worse nutrition (huge snowball) and then ... break-down (kaboom).

Chronic stress can lead to anxiety. Even though both terms are used interchangeably, there are subtle differences between them. While stress works well at motivating you to finish tasks, study for exams, and turn up to class, anxiety actually *stops* you from finishing tasks, or studying for exams or turning up to class. It's usually far more persistent; lingering on even when the stressor is no longer there. Anxiety is a feeling of apprehension or fear and the source of this fear is not always known or recognised, which can add to the distress you feel.

A scan through the synonyms for the word 'anxiety' is interesting: worry, fear, agitation, nervousness, unease, disquiet, angst. Collectively they can all contribute to anxiety, but are so closely associated with it, that it's hard to distinguish between them. It's much like the "uncomfortable paradox." Stress can trigger anxiety, and anxiety can make stress feel more intense, eventually building that giant snowball of *increased* stress and *increased* anxiety that can be difficult to escape.

The snowball analogy is appropriate but not quite accurate. Snowballs form quite fast, but stress and anxiety can (and often does) develop *gradually*. There is a theory that if a frog is put suddenly into boiling water, it will jump out. But if it's put in water which is at room temperature, and then the temperature is gradually increased, the frog won't perceive the danger and eventually will be boiled alive. This is not a theory I'd ever want to test, as I quite like frogs. In reality, if the water got too hot, the frog would simply jump out.

#2. The best way to stop a giant snowball forming is not to roll it down the hill in the first place.

There are many times when the environment around us changes and we don't really notice the gradual shift. You get to bed 15 minutes later one night, then another 15 minutes the next. Eventually your 8 hours of sleep has been eroded to six. You skip a few meals, and before you know it breakfast becomes a coffee and lunch is non-existent. It's very easy to do. You work a little longer on your essay, go out less, stress more and within a few weeks you realise that you've hardly been out with your friends and exercise is a distant memory. The important thing is to recognise is when stress has tipped over into something more serious. This is the point where, like the frog, you need to jump out of the water before it gets too hot.

The perfect storm

Imagine your task was to design the perfect setting for stress and anxiety to flourish. How about we create a really competitive environment throw in the prospect of constant evaluations, assessments and exams, add high expectations and pressure to perform, and then make you pay for the whole experience. Is it any wonder that students are more prone to stress and anxiety than the general population?

It's something I don't want to make light of because, while the figures vary by country, educational system, and age group, research consistently shows that simply being a student is a significant contributor to poor mental health. Survey after survey has a majority of students rating their mental health as only fair or poor, with up to 65% finding their academic experiences in general to be 'very' or 'extremely stressful'. Most students felt overwhelming anxiety at some point during the academic year with over 20% being diagnosed or treated for depression. Many students reported stress so severe it negatively impacted their academic performance. In one survey half the students reported feeling isolated due to academic pressures limiting their social relationships. There seems to be no avoiding the fact that study can be stressful.

As a lecturer, I wanted to find out first hand exactly what things were causing my students to be stressed.

WHAT STRESS ISN'T

For six semesters, in every one of my classes I asked students to spend 10 minutes writing down "what type of things related to study cause you stress." The students were not restricted in how they should respond. Most wrote their list in point form, while others wrote in full sentences and paragraphs, relating often poignant stories about just how stressful study was to them. Some lists were only a handful of dot points, while others were twenty or more. Very few students had little to say. Most wrote easily and without any prompting.

The majority of students were between 18 and 25 years old, studying full-time – some straight from school and quite a few returning to study after a period of work. There of course were also mature age students, many looking for a change in career late in life. Every semester, I would add the responses to a cumulative spreadsheet. Out of close to 1,500 responses, a very clear pattern emerged, with students' concerns centring around four main issues: time management, dealing with deadlines, performing well, and the fear of failure.

The stressor that was usually at the top of the list was, balancing a heavy academic workload with extracurricular activities, part-time jobs, and personal commitments. Financial considerations such as tuition fees and the general cost of living (particularly for students away from home) made this balancing act even more precarious.

Academia is built around exams, assignments, and presentations, so it's no surprise that students were concerned about meeting deadlines and dealing with the inevitable procrastination which in turn creates a cycle of last-minute cramming, and increasing anxiety (think snowball). This is one stressor that virtually all respondents noted in my survey.

The need to achieve was clearly demonstrated in the responses. Students found their desire to be "doing well" and "getting good grades" stressful. No matter whether we are studying or not, we are constantly being evaluated. We undergo performance reviews at work, receive 'likes' and comments on social media, people comment on how we look, and financial institutions evaluate our net worth. However, rarely are the results of any evaluation presented as starkly as in the education system, where every exam, quiz or assessment is marked and graded. The pressure to succeed can become overwhelming, particularly when it feels like failure is simply not an option. So, not only is there pressure to do well, there is even more pressure to "not fail." The fear of disappointing others only increases the stakes.

Of course there were a host of other concerns – everything from in-class presentations to the fear of not finding work after graduation. The whole study experience based on these statistics would seem to be a rather grim undertaking, but intuitively I know that not to be the case. I have had the good fortune of being able to hand students their degrees at graduation, and the pride of achievement is palpable. It's a happy event – the culmination of an academic journey with a tangible reward at the end.

A cautionary caveat when considering the statistics related to academic stress is that study on the whole can at times be a stressful experience. To that extent, a certain level of stress is accepted, and even expected; however, chronic conditions such as anxiety and depression should not be part of that experience. The goal is not to eliminate all stress (that would be virtually impossible) but to find appropriate ways to deal with it.

The human cost of academic anxiety

As a lecturer, one of the things I prided myself on was being able to build a good rapport with my students. One particular Wednesday night class was no exception. I had been teaching for about 10 years, so was quite confident and comfortable. Jenny was a bright and friendly student who would often stay back after class to ask for more clarification on something we'd covered, or to get more details on her assessments. At first it was an imposition, because I was eager to get home to have dinner, or perhaps watch something on television with my wife. Eventually I just accepted that Jenny was a dedicated student keen to do well.

I would normally arrive 10 to 15 minutes earlier to set up for the lecture. We were about half way through the semester, and the first of the major assessments were due. The pre-class set up for me usually involved friendly banter with the students who were arriving after work. I noticed this evening that the mood was a little more sombre. One of the students approached me and asked, "Can I talk to you for a minute?" This was not at all unusual for this time of year so I was getting ready for the standard extension request.

The student was a little awkward, "It's about Jenny," he said. "She took her own life last week. I just thought you should know." I can't remember exactly what my first thought was, but there was certainly gratitude that the student told me before class had started. Jenny was always one of the first to arrive and was never absent, so imagine if I would have made some sort of flippant remark. I was shocked, of course, but it never really dawned on me how self-centred my reaction was.

The lecture was surreal because for all intents and purposes, I ran the class just like any other, and was still being as good humoured as I always was - it was business as usual. I'm a professional, I thought. But over the coming weeks I was plagued by feelings of guilt. Should I have known? Was there something I missed? Is there any way I could have seen this happening? Was it the assessment? Could I have said something? Did I listen to her concerns enough?

As with so many of these cases, Jenny had no history of mental illness, and as far as I knew this was a complete shock to her family and friends. The student who approached me before class was Jenny's colleague and her good friend. He told me Jenny was very popular, a high achiever, very competent at work, and good at most things she attempted. I nodded in recognition of a back-story so familiar. A high-achieving student, struggling under the burden of high expectations, anything less than perfection is failure. Grades that once came easily become harder to maintain. Anxiety and self-doubt creep in, the usual methods of coping, such as studying harder and isolating from friends, only make things worse. Thoughts of inadequacy begin to spiral out of control, along with a growing sense of hopelessness.

I will never know what drove Jenny to do what she did, but the thought that it may have had something to do with study was in some ways the genesis of this book. How can something that is meant to be enriching and uplifting cause a person to suffer so much that they can see no other way out. In countries with particularly competitive education systems, like Japan, South Korea, China, and India, the rates of student suicides attributed to academic anxiety are high. The statistics related to young people taking their own lives primarily as a result of academic stress makes for sombre reading.

Until now, I have never really acknowledged, discussed or written about what happened with Jenny, even though ultimately it had such an impact on my career as a lecturer. It changed the way I approached teaching. I did everything in my power to lessen the academic burden on my students. If extensions were needed, they were granted, no questions asked. I rarely enforced the late penalty, unless absolutely necessary; it's only study, after all. It wasn't unusual for me to give the entire class extra time on an assessment if I could see they were struggling with deadlines. I spent a lot of time in class discussing and defusing the stress often associated with study. Not only did it define my teaching style, it hopefully contributed to the well-being of my students.

I now realise that Jenny not only had a lasting impact on me as a teacher, but she also played a part in the development of this book. If this book is able to help just one student, then the effort of writing it will have been totally worthwhile.

3. PSYCHOBABBLE

> The great revolution of our generation is the discovery that human beings, by changing the inner attitudes of their minds, can change the outer aspects of their lives.
>
> *William James*
> *American philosopher and psychologist*

Defusing a bomb

I love the scene in any action movie where the hero has to try and defuse a bomb. It's usually a collection of coloured wires in a tangled confusing mass, with the red digital read-out of the timer relentlessly counting down the seconds. There are two directions this scene can go. In one, after an agonising delay, our hero <sweat beading on their forehead> considers which wire to cut <music builds to a tense crescendo> … then, snip … the timer stops and everybody breathes a sigh of relief; disaster averted. The other scenario sees the hero cut the wire, but the clock keeps ticking. Now the only solution is to run to the edge of the <bridge, boat, cliff or

crevasse> and throw the bomb into the abyss. The bomb explodes in the distance and everybody breathes a sigh of relief; disaster averted.

You're probably way ahead of me, and have worked out that stress and anxiety can be much like the bomb (a collection of coloured wires in a tangled confusing mass). The big question is, do you try and defuse it, or do you (figuratively speaking) 'throw the bomb into the abyss'. Actually, there is a third scenario, but I doubt you'd see it very often in the movies: the hero just hopes for the best and calmly lets the bomb explode. There is a lot of merit to the "not giving a stuff" approach, but it's a very hard thing to do when you're standing in the shattered remains of your exam results.

Throwing the bomb into the abyss is essentially the same as not sitting for an upcoming exam – you're simply removing the stressor. But that would mean failing your unit, so the only realistic option in this case is to defuse the bomb. This scenario delivers us headlong into the realm of psychology where defusing bombs is all in a days work. Psychology is essentially the scientific study of the mind and behaviour. The golden formula of all things psychological is centred on three fundamental elements, the affective, behavioural and cognitive aspects of being human. In plain English: our feelings, our actions and our thoughts. What makes psychology so interesting is that all humans experience all three, and all three are interconnected.

The term 'cognitive' refers to anything to do with thinking; things such as reasoning, problem-solving, decision-making, memory, and perception. Affective (feeling) involves our emotions and moods, which influence how we feel about situations, people, and ourselves. Behavioural is all about what we do; so basically any observable action. In fact, behaviour is the only element we can actually see; the other two may require some detective-work to figure out. We can't really see someone's thoughts or feelings but we do get clues – sometimes very obvious ones such as crying or laughing, for example.

Picture this scenario. The results have just been released for a recent exam. Three friends are incredulous to discover that they've received exactly the same grade: 68/100, a credit. James is thrilled. He jumps up and down, and fist-pumps the air "Wooo! This is great. I can't believe it." His best friend Josh, collapses in a heap, shoulder slumped, hands clasped on head, "This is a terrible mark," he cries, "what a disaster!" Julie gets her grade, smiles, shrugs and gets ready for an afternoon spent surfing.

For James, getting a credit was a personal triumph. It was a subject he wasn't keen on, but he'd spent quite a bit of time studying – more than he usually would. His behaviour gives us a good indication as to how pleased he is. He doesn't have to repeat the unit, he is one step closer to getting his qualification, and the effort he put in was worthwhile … it's a good outcome.

Julie was not too stressed about her marks. Her thoughts are more focussed on travel and having fun. She enrolled to study primarily because her friends were there, and on some days catching a good wave was way more important than study. Julie spent a few hours revising but the exam wasn't high on her priority list and she was definitely pleased with her grade.

So the same mark resulted in very different cognitive, emotional and behavioural responses. It's no surprise, because every single person on the planet is different; the combination of our experiences, memories, attitudes, opinions and beliefs are all unique. No one can have the exact same set of memories that you have. That is a fascinating thing to ponder, especially since there are so many ways in which we, as humans, are all the same.

Deconstructing Josh

But what about Josh? It is immediately clear, judging by his body language that something is wrong (collapsing in a heap, shoulders slumped, hands clasped on head), and if that isn't enough, then lamenting, "This is a terrible mark, what a disaster," should be a fairly obvious clue. Why the difference in reaction?

Josh's family always had high expectations for him. His mother is a doctor; his father works in finance. Josh is a high achiever, with his sights set on corporate law. He would like to intern at one of the more prestigious law firms, and to reach this goal he needs a distinction grade as an average. So a credit is indeed a setback. In Josh's family, top grades were celebrated and rewarded - the more impressive the achievement, the better the reward. But failure also had its consequences. When he was at school, Josh did badly in one of his major exams and it was a big deal. Apart from the general air of disappointment, he wasn't allowed to play his favourite computer game for a week.

The concept of reinforcement as a consequence of behaviour is at the heart of operant conditioning and quite often at the core of how and why we react to certain situation in the way we do. The most significant individual in this field was psychologist, B. F. Skinner who used rats, pigeons, boxes, levers, lights and a few amps of electricity here and there to demonstrate his theories.

In Josh's case, his parents (intentionally or not), were influencing his behaviour through positive or negative reinforcement or punishment. It gets a little confusing because in the world of operant conditioning, positive does not necessarily mean a good, and negative is not necessarily bad. Positive means adding something, and negative means taking something away. Reward means you are increasing behaviour, while punishment means decreasing behaviour.

In less time than you may think, associations are formed in the brain, between academic performance and self worth. If I do well at school, my parents are pleased with me, so I've made them happy. If I do badly, I've disappointed them. I'm not a good son or daughter because I've let them down. For Josh, an upcoming exam becomes far more than a simple test of knowledge and understanding; it morphs into a way of proving his affection for his parents.

On the day of the exam (whether he consciously realises it or not) Josh perceives the exam as a threat and thanks to the "fight or flight" response releases a huge dose of the hormone adrenaline. His body can't tell whether the threat is real or not – it is merely responding to the signals his brain is giving out. And although he isn't actually running or fighting, thanks to the adrenaline his mouth goes dry, it's hard to concentrate, and panic sets in. Even so, the long hours of study pay off, and Josh manages to get a decent mark, but for him it's perceived as a "disaster."

Josh's credit grade, by any standard, is a good grade. Considering he found himself stressed and panicked during the exam, it was a remarkable effort. Rather than worry about the lost marks, he should celebrate the solid performance. There is room for improvement, but he had studied consistently, and essentially completed the exam under pressure. Sometimes the key to changing our attitudes is reframing what our perception of success is.

Cognitive restructuring

The Alan Parsons Project was a British 'progressive rock' band who produced 10 studio albums between 1975 and 1990. Their 1982 album, *Eye in the Sky*, features a song titled "Psychobabble" which was about the often confusing language used in fields such as psychology and psychiatry. 'Cognitive restructuring', is probably a good example. The term refers to a therapeutic technique used in cognitive-behavioural therapy (CBT) to help a person identify, challenge, and change negative or distorted thought patterns. The core idea is that our thoughts (cognitive) influence how we feel and how we behave, and by changing unhelpful patterns of thinking, we can improve emotional well-being and change behaviour. That's not always an easy task.

The way we think about things has been built up gradually over many years, so that by the time we are young adults, our life experiences and the things we have learned create a unique way of viewing the world and ourselves. We become comfortable with our way of thinking because that's what we've become used to.

Luckily when it comes to identifying thought patterns, some of the work has been done for us. Welcome to the world of cognitive distortions. These are irrational or biased ways of thinking that can lead to increased stress, anxiety, and frustration (especially when it comes to studying). They are very closely related to cognitive biases. Both deal with thinking errors, but the consequences of cognitive distortions usually lead to negative or harmful thought patterns (whereas a cognitive bias is just that … a bias).

#3. The key to changing a negative thought pattern is to recognise that it is in fact, negative.

Psychologists have identified several types of cognitive distortions, each with a distinct pattern of thought, and a name to categorise it. 'All-or-Nothing Thinking' (or 'Black-and-White Thinking'), for example, is seeing things in extreme terms, like either a total success or a complete failure, with no middle ground. "If I don't get an A on this exam, I'm a total failure." There is, of course, no logic to that thought. If you didn't get top marks, you simply didn't get top marks.

Students will sometimes jump to an incorrect conclusion based on a single event or experience. "I didn't do well on this quiz, so now I'm going to fail the entire course." Then they somehow manage to further escalate that thought to a catastrophic outcome, "I'll never graduate, and my future will be ruined." That's called catastrophising.

When we process information, it is easier to take a 'mental short-cut' rather than analyse and process all the possible logical alternatives. The psychobabble term for these short-cuts is 'mental heuristics'. The problem is that without sufficient analysis, the conclusion may well be incorrect. "I'm going to fail the exam no matter how hard I study." You've suddenly become a fortune teller, and are now predicting something that hasn't happened (and probably won't happen).

"It's not fair that everybody else seems to understand the material so easily, and I don't. I'll never catch up." What evidence do you have that "everybody else" understands the material easily? Why do you think you won't be able to catch up? "The teacher didn't say anything, so they probably think I'm dumb." This is 'mind reading', assuming you know what others are thinking, often in a negative way, and again, without evidence. The key word here (and with all the distortions) is *evidence*.

When I was in my mid-twenties, I went on a short road-trip to Surfers Paradise (in Queensland, Australia) with two of my closest friends, Steve and John. The discussion in the car turned to one of our favourite albums, *Grafitti Crimes* by New Zealand band Mi-Sex. This was a vinyl LP, of course, as music streaming wasn't really a thing back then. For over 2 hours John and I argued about which track the song "Computer Games" was on the album. To settle the debate we drove 100 kilometres out of our way to find a music store so we could determine who was right (Google wasn't a thing back then either). We needed conclusive evidence. And that is exactly what is generally needed when dealing with cognitive distortions – evidence.

When faced with a cognitive distortion, gathering evidence allows you to challenge each thought, to question its validity, examine the arguments for and against, and consider an alternative perspective. Now you can reframe the original negative thought into a more balanced and rational thought. This doesn't necessarily mean forcing overly positive thinking but rather, finding a healthier, more accurate perspective.

Hope for the best

People have always wanted to be happy. It has been a central theme in philosophy, religion, and human endeavour across cultures for thousands of years. It was a talking point for the Greek philosophers Socrates, Plato, and especially Aristotle who rated happiness as one of the greatest goals humans can achieve. English philosopher, John Stuart Mill, proposed that the goal of society should be the greatest happiness for the greatest number of people. It is even enshrined in the *U.S. Declaration of Independence*, where Thomas Jefferson declared the right to "life, liberty, and the pursuit of happiness." But what exactly is happiness?

While the modern understanding of "happiness" is usually linked to personal well-being, contentment, and fulfilment, earlier conceptions tied happiness to virtue, divine will, or communal good. With the science of psychology gaining traction in the early 20th century, William James (often credited as the 'father of modern psychology') wrote about "healthy mindedness". Carl Jung explored how mental attitudes influence behaviour and well-being, and the often quoted Abraham Maslow developed the concept of "self actualisation" as a way of reaching one's full potential. The focus slowly started to shift from happiness to positivity.

In the mid 1950s Norman Vincent Peale wrote *The Power of Positive Thinking*, which became one of the most influential and best-selling self-help books of all time. Peale was inspired by the belief that our thoughts shape our reality. He began promoting the idea that optimism and positive thinking could not only improve mental health but also lead to success in people's personal and professional lives.

A Google search on the term "positive psychology" delivered 330 million hits in 0.58 seconds. The scope and breadth of positivity is staggering: apart from diplomas, degrees, seminars, interventions, and conferences; positive programs have been embraced by schools, universities, the corporate sector, and even within governmental policy. The 'father of the positive psychology movement' is esteemed psychologist, Martin Seligman. His light-bulb moment was realising that modern psychology had developed into a discipline that mainly aimed to solve problems, and to that extent was focussing on negative things. Why not focus on the things that contribute positively to our well-being and happiness? What are our strengths rather than our weaknesses? How do we get the most out of our lives? It was a simple matter of reframing: don't focus on what you can't do. Focus on what you *can* do.

A new vocabulary developed and words such as flourishing, flow and grit took on new meanings. To flourish was to thrive in life, experience a sense of purpose, growth, and positive engagement. 'Flow' morphed into a nifty descriptor for a state of absorption or being really "into something." It's not a new phenomenon, with artists, writers, musicians, and people form all walks of life, having described something similar for decades. The word 'grit' became synonymous for resilience, which in itself became a fundamental tenet of the positive psychology movement.

One of our family's favourite movies is the Mel Brooks film, *The Twelve Chairs* - viewing it is virtually a yearly event. The song "Hope for the Best (Expect the Worst)" plays during the film's opening credits. I couldn't think of a better phrase than that to reflect a mindset which balances optimism with realism. It suggests you can certainly be hopeful for positive outcomes but nonetheless prepare for potential difficulties. The pressure to maintain constant positivity can feel overwhelming, especially when you are already dealing with stress and high expectations. The idea that you must always "stay positive" just adds another layer of pressure. Instead, simply aiming to avoid negativity may be a healthier and more realistic approach for many.

#4. There are times when there may be no obvious positives; this is when simply 'not being negative' is good enough.

Instead of forcing yourself to be positive, you can allow yourself to acknowledge any disappointment or frustration you feel about a particular grade without any judgment. It's perfectly normal to feel this way, and recognising these emotions without being consumed by them is important. Personally, when I just focus on avoiding a negative outlook, I can process things at my own pace, without feeling burdened by unrealistic expectations of happiness or positivity.

Food for thought

For most of us, our day is divided into three roughly equal chunks: sleeping, working and leisure. Depending on your circumstances, study may fit somewhere within your work time or leisure time, or perhaps both. We need sleep and nutrition to stay alive and exercise is optional, but highly recommended. Prioritising these three elements is an often neglected part of understanding emotional well-being. The quickest way to change how you feel is to change what you do.

It's so obvious, isn't it? Eat well, get enough sleep and exercise regularly. I can almost feel the collective eye-roll. But, when it comes to sleep, exercise and nutrition, most studies indicate students are particularly neglectful of all three. To quote Morpheus, from the film *The Matrix*: "knowing the path is not the same as walking it." Studies suggest that many students experience poor sleep quality, sleep deprivation and irregular sleep schedules. When it comes to exercise, researchers reported that about 40% to 50% of college students are physically inactive. A major Australian survey concluded that as secondary school students advance in year levels, their fruit and vegetable intake reduces while their consumption of soft drink and fast food increases. It's no surprise, as marketers of fast food and energy drinks actively target the student population.

So here I am, sitting in a food court outside of a Donut King franchise, munching on a fresh, hot cinnamon donut, as I write about healthy eating. The irony of the situation doesn't escape me. I'm a Type 1 diabetic, so I've had to dose extra insulin to eat the donut, and even that isn't going to keep my blood sugar under control. But in my defence, it's a rare indulgence.

The diabetes forces me to constantly be aware of what I eat, and monitor the carbohydrates I consume. Very low blood sugar affects the way you think and process information (something I've discovered first hand), as the brain depends on glucose to function. The process of study puts extra demands on your brain. Healthy and nutritious meals help maintain consistent energy levels throughout the day, and provide essential nutrients and vitamins that enhance memory, and improve cognitive function.

Unfortunately, for many students, processed foods, convenience meals, coffee and energy drinks form the foundation of their diet. There is no harm in the occasional treat (written while munching on the remaining bites of my donut), but as a rule, healthy eating is the first of three behavioural goals that will make life as a student so much easier.

Getting a good night's sleep should be another goal. Adequate sleep helps regulate the body's stress response; making you more resilient to academic pressures ('adequate' is between 7 to 9 hours). Lack of sleep has detrimental effects on your cognitive function, memory, and mood. It's harder to function at a peak level when you're tired. It's as simple as that. Sleep is crucial for memory consolidation, the process by which short-term memories are transformed into long-term ones. Without enough sleep, it's more difficult to retain information learned during study sessions.

The third goal is getting regular exercise. Physical activity increases blood flow to the brain, which improves cognitive function, including memory, attention, and processing speed. Exercise releases endorphins, the body's natural stress-relieving hormones, which can help reduce anxiety and improve mood, making it easier to focus on studying. According to most official medical and government institutions the target for adults should be about 30 minutes of moderate aerobic activity (like brisk walking, cycling, or swimming) at least 5 days a week.

I swim 10 laps most days at the university pool. 'Swimming' may be a generous term, as without my flippers and hand-paddles I would most likely sink. One of the lifeguards, Marcus, swam 120 laps (a mind-numbing 6 kilometres) 6 days a week when training. He was an elite athlete having competed at a national level. We often chat about the benefits of swimming. For Marcus, it's not just a way to keep physically fit, but it is something that kept him grounded and focussed while he was studying. My daughter Emily is also a pretty decent swimmer averaging 1 kilometre most days, summer and winter. For her, swimming is not only a way of achieving physical well-being, but also maintaining emotional well-being.

Anyone who has tried to eat better, or do more exercise, or get to bed earlier will appreciate that it can be a lot harder than it seems. So how do you go from 'knowing the path' to walking it? The answer is: the same way you defuse that bomb; slowly and carefully.

Some people may be able to change their behaviour in an instant. In one giant burst of motivation, they start exercising, change their entire diet, and start sleeping a regular 8 hours each night. It's possible, but quite rare. For most people it's best to change things gradually. Your body needs time to get used to changes in your diet. Sleep patterns take time to adjust. Eat one less fast food meal a week, get to bed 15 minutes earlier every night, walk 50 metres more every day. When compounded over time, small consistent changes can lead to significant major changes and completely transform where we end up.

4. THE EDUCATION SYSTEM

The fact is that given the challenges we face, education doesn't need to be reformed — it needs to be transformed. The key is not to standardise education, but to personalise it, to build achievement on discovering the talents of each child, to put students in an environment where they want to learn and where they can naturally discover their true passions.

Sir Ken Robinson
British author, international advisor on education

Prison and preschool

While the comparison may sound harsh, there are a surprising number of similarities between the education system and the prison system – at least that's what springs to mind when I think of my own schooling. Both include a defined period of time where freedom is completely ignored; both have a dress code, an authoritarian structure, set times, and usually no input in decision making.

THE EDUCATION SYSTEM

The salient point is that for most of the world, there is a period in one's life where education is compulsory. There are only a handful of countries where this is not the case. A majority of children begin their formal education in Kindergarten between 4 and 6 years of age, and end it when they are between 17 or 18 years old. While the exact number of years can vary, the general standard world-wide is around 12 years. There are government schools, non-government schools and independent schools. Educational policies can range from quite strict and formal to the more flexible and holistic models such as the Montessori and Steiner systems. Some schools are based on religious preference while others, such as performing arts schools are based on aptitude.

We progress through the system in a fairly structured manner. Pre-primary education is designed to support a child's development in preparation for school life, focussing on fundamental skills such as reading, writing and mathematics. Secondary education is typically more subject-oriented and aims to establish a solid foundation for learning at a tertiary level. For the most part, that is the extent of formal compulsory schooling. Students are then released into the real world to fend for themselves.

The boundaries between each level of education usually results in some degree of stress. I certainly remember the transition from primary school to secondary school. My uniform was different; I had to travel by train; there were new teachers; and now I was able to choose which subjects I studied. Then as a senior we graduated from a blue shirt to white, and added a red tie. We were now the "leaders of the school;" young adults about to embark on the journey of our life.

For some reason (and it's virtually a global phenomenon) for many students, the final year of high school will be the most stressful time of their academic life. Apart from the harsh realisation that this year is the culmination of your formal schooling, there is a legion of exams and assessments that usually determine whether you will be accepted into your university of choice.

But what a cruel convergence of factors: students at this point are usually around 17 or 18 years old; it's the time when their social activity hits its peak; independence and freedom become very important; and part-time work becomes more prominent. This is the worst possible time to sit a formal exam. In the UK students study for their GCEs (general certificate of education), in the USA, students sit their SATs (Scholastic Aptitude Test), and for Australian students it's the HSC (Higher School Certificate) which results in an ATAR (Australian Tertiary Admission Rank). You are now released on good behaviour, free to take on the world. For many, that will include more study.

THE EDUCATION SYSTEM

Depending on the vocation you choose, your educational journey may continue in new and unexpected ways. Exactly what that path looks like will depend on the career you pursue. Some professions require multiple qualifications. For instance, becoming a surgeon not only requires a medical degree, but also additional specialised study and training in surgery.

Freshman and sophomores

I grew up on a steady diet of American television shows from the 1970's – *The Brady Bunch* being one of them. It was my introduction to the American college culture; complete with prom nights, cheerleaders, glee clubs, and fraternity houses. My only wish at the time was to own a letterman jacket. A proliferation of 'frat movies' (the 1978 classic, *Animal House* springs immediately to mind) only reinforced my perception of university life.

The now familiar terms freshmen, sophomores, juniors and seniors originated in the UK within their eminent universities, Oxford and Cambridge, and were adopted in the United States by Harvard around the mid 17th century. So, a freshman is a first year university student, a sophomore is in their second year, and junior and senior are the third and fourth years respectively.

The term sophomore has quite an interesting history. The Greek word for clever or wise is *sophos*, and the one for foolish is *moros* ... so literally it means, "wise fools." These words perfectly sum up my first few years as a university student which was a combination of sheer laziness and sheer brilliance. Having come from a structured school system where for the better part of 12 years my weekdays had been divided up into neatly compartmentalised 'periods', the sudden freedom university life offered was overwhelming. There were lectures which weren't (strictly speaking) compulsory, and tutorials which were compulsory but 'lenient' if you were absent. There were new friendship groups, food courts, countless clubs and societies you could join, and there was the Uni Bar. Study was a necessary evil which one had to suffer though in order to enjoy all the trappings of university life.

Tertiary education is usually the domain of universities and colleges. In this book I use the terms interchangeably, however technically, there are some differences. Most universities typically offer both undergraduate and graduate degrees; they tend to be large institutions with different 'schools' or faculties, such as the School of Arts, the Faculty of Science, and so on. Colleges are usually smaller in size and they tend not to offer as many majors and programs as universities. Typically colleges don't grant post-graduate degrees, however there are many exceptions to that rule.

If wading your way through the terminology seems daunting, don't worry, you're not alone. Undergraduate, postgraduate, diploma, graduate diploma; there are a lot of different qualifications. Let's start with the bachelor's degree as it's probably the most common university qualification and is recognised worldwide. This is usually 3 to 4 years of study at an *undergraduate* level. The logic here is that you haven't graduated yet; so a bachelor's degree is an undergraduate degree. When you finish your study, you are still technically not a graduate ... yet. The Academic Board of the college or university needs to confer the degree, which essentially means you now have the green light to graduate. The graduation ceremony is usually where you receive your testamur, which is the document that most students get framed and put on their wall.

There are many undergraduate qualifications such as certificates and diplomas, which are commonly delivered by TAFE colleges (in Australia), community education centres and private RTO's (Registered Training Organisations). Certificates and diplomas are accepted by universities to be the equivalent of six to twelve months of a Bachelor's degree in a related field of study.

Degrees that are higher than the bachelor's level are classed as postgraduate. These include master's and doctoral degrees, graduate certificates and graduate diplomas. Completing a degree at the doctoral level means you can use the title Doctor. Honours may be awarded atop a bachelor's degree after an additional year of study for three-year degrees. Once you graduate you get to use whatever letters you've earned after your name (they're called post-nominals). They will vary depending on your course, but like so much else in academia, there is quite a protocol surrounding their use. Generally you only use your post-nominals in an educational or professional context.

While the majority of students attend public universities and colleges, private universities account for quite a significant proportion of enrolments. It's probably stating the obvious, but the most prestigious universities are usually the most popular, the most expensive and also the most competitive to get in to. But the competition doesn't end there – the universities also compete against each other. Factors such as general reputation and research output combine to arrive at a world ranking, which as one would imagine, has a significant impact on the international prestige of a particular institution.

The business of education

There is no way to escape the fact that education is big business. Countries like the USA, UK, and Australia actively market their higher education systems to international students. With the growth of online study and e-learning platforms, education has become a lucrative global industry. Many universities behave exactly like big corporations, generating revenue through endowments, fundraising, and sports programs. In the USA, for example, college sports are a billion-dollar industry, with schools profiting from ticket sales, broadcasting rights, and merchandising. Many of the larger universities generate additional revenue through intellectual property developed from faculty research, often leading to patents, partnerships with industries, and spin-off companies (Google and its development at Stanford University is a prime example).

When my children were all at school age, our single biggest household expense was school fees (and orthodontics). Education at all levels represents a significant financial investment for parents and then eventually for the students themselves. The average cost of university education varies significantly based on the country, type of institution, field of study, and whether scholarships or government support are available. For many students, higher education can easily become one of the most expensive endeavours they can undertake. There are tuition fees, student amenities fees, parking, textbooks, peripherals such as laptops, food, on-campus accommodation; it's a considerable amount. No matter how you look at it, education is a big investment in terms of time and money, but it's a very worthwhile one.

Most education 'systems' need some form of administration, an educational program of study (a curriculum), and people to teach it. Where schools have principals and vice principals, most universities and colleges have chancellors, vice-chancellors, registrars and deans. The teachers at universities are usually tutors and lecturers, with the more senior staff being senior lecturers or professors.

Universities and colleges are required to report to various governing bodies and regulators in order to remain registered. Each course that is offered will have been vetted and endorsed by a variety of committees consisting of senior academics, educators and experts in their field. Every course will have a set number of units that need to be completed in order to gain the qualification you have enrolled in. Each unit will have a specific set of criteria that has to be met in order to gain a passing mark. This is set out in a syllabus or unit outline which usually identifies a series of learning outcomes that must be met.

Determining exactly how those outcomes will be met is where things like assessments and exams come in; they are designed to measure knowledge, skill, competency, and understanding. As you can imagine, there is much debate surrounding the best way to do this. Once a student has passed the required number of units, they are awarded the qualification.

Publish or perish

The academic world is an interesting place. Since the origins of universities late in the 11th century, some things have changed drastically while others have changed very little. Go to any graduation ceremony, and you will be transported back into an era of colourful robes, funny hats and arcane traditions. Like a majority of large organisations, a university is structured and hierarchical. A junior academic can find themselves tutoring classes, then becoming a lecturer, a senior lecturer, then associate professor, then professor, and finally retiring to a nice little villa in Italy (Spain, France, Portugal, take your pick) with the well earned title of Emeritus Professor. As I often say, "it's a good gig."

Unlike many other career paths, success in academia depends largely on your research and publications. If you were an academic that focussed mainly on the teaching (like I was) moving up the ladder could be a little trickier. There isn't that much room for lazy researchers (like me). The well known aphorism "publish or perish," sums up the situation nicely. Universities, like businesses, compete for rankings and prestige, which are both enhanced by research output.

In academia, being cited is a big thing. In fact it's all about citations. You write a 'paper' and the aim is to have it published in a journal. Even though there are thousands of scholarly journals (estimates range between

30,000 and 80,000), publishing literally millions of articles each year, the process is still quite a competitive. The more important and prestigious the journal, the more competitive it is, and the better it is for the academic (and the university) to be represented. It's not much different to a journalist who aspires to have their story accepted by the *New York Times* or *Washington Post*.

#5. The best way to sound smart is to reference someone smarter.

The bedrock of all academic publishing is the peer-review system. This is a process used to evaluate the originality, validity, significance and quality of research before it is published in scholarly journals. So, an author submits their manuscript to a journal for consideration, the manuscript is reviewed by a number of selected experts in the field who recommend whether to publish it or not. Students around the world are taught that citing peer-reviewed journals is essential for maintaining the integrity, credibility, and rigor of academic work.

While peer review remains the gold standard in academic publishing, there are quite a few issues surrounding it that suggest the system is not without its challenges. Some critics feel that there is a bias towards research from well-known institutions or well known authors. Depending on the review process there can be a lack of transparency. In a 'single-blind' review (which is one of the more common) the reviewers know who the authors are, but the authors do not know who the reviewers are. Other critics point out that research with a successful outcome is more likely to be published, even though it can be argued that failed research can be just as interesting.

Algebra in the coffee lounge

The quote opening this chapter is by Sir Ken Robinson who is a well known British author, speaker, and international advisor on education in the arts. His main argument is that modern education systems, often emphasise conformity, standardisation, and academic achievement, rather than fostering individual talents, creativity, and holistic development. No doubt this would be a mantra echoed by advocates of the Montessori and Steiner styles of education where the uniqueness of each student is celebrated, and learning is structured around their strengths, passions, and interests. Sadly, this is not always the case in traditional education.

In Year 8, my daughter, Emily, decided she no longer wanted to go to school. It was not defiance; it was a genuine overwhelming anxiety. This will pass, I thought somewhat naively. 'School refusal' is certainly not unheard of. There is quite a bit of literature on it, and as you might imagine many strategies designed to help. The problem is that the success of these strategies is greatly aided by the school being supportive and empathetic. Emily attended an independent girl's school which unfortunately was far from being supportive or empathetic. When the frontline strategies of cajoling and encouragement failed, they moved into a 'colour-by-numbers' version of positive education, closely followed by veiled threats of academic suspension.

We had reached an impasse, and after a particularly frustrating and distressing exchange with the school, decided that home-schooling would be the best option. Our plan initially was to only do it for 6 months and then reassess the situation. Home schooling is probably not suitable for everyone, but in Emily's case it was perfect. She thrived. It was everything education should be: personalised hands-on learning, skills-based tasks, excursions, and algebra in many different coffee lounges complete with a hot chocolate and cake (I so wish that were my schooling). Admittedly, Emily was a motivated and enthusiastic student. Our six month trial turned into two and a half years, and it was without doubt the best educational experience I have ever been involved in.

I even invented a subject for her: People, Places, Ideas and Events (PPIE); we called it "pippy" for short. It was a subject I wish I had at school, spanning everything from science, geography, history, philosophy and the arts. What Emily achieved is a credit to her, but an indictment on a school that was completely ill-equipped to deal with anything outside the norm. Our experience with Emily led me to focus more on the question of what does formal education actually offer.

Some schools, universities and colleges, could certainly do better. They preside over a system that at times prioritises test results over deeper learning, creativity, and critical thinking. This can lead to a "teach to the test" culture, where students may excel in exams but struggle with applying knowledge in real-world situations. Students can have diverse learning styles and a variety of interests, but traditional education tends to follow a one-size-fits-all approach, resulting in some students feeling left behind, while others are not challenged enough.

#6. It's important to remember, the goal of education isn't just academic achievement; it's helping you discover who you are and who you want to become.

In some cases the curriculum is outdated, and fails to reflect advances in technology or the field of study. Students may not be encouraged to think independently or solve problems creatively. Some methods of assessment are unimaginative and repetitive. There can be a lack of creativity and innovation in the way content is delivered – with students often being presented with large slabs of information crammed onto a presentation slide.

We are all unique in the way we learn and approach study. We bring different strengths, face different challenges, and pursue goals that reflect our unique interests. You might be naturally gifted at solving complex problems, or your talents may lie in creative expression. Some students thrive with hands-on tasks, while others prefer reading, listening, or learning through discussion. For some, the academic world feels like a second home; for others, it can be a daunting and unfamiliar place. Whatever your experience, understanding how you learn best is the key to making study work for you.

5. KNOWLEDGE & LEARNING

In times of change, learners inherit the earth, while the learned find themselves beautifully equipped to deal with a world that no longer exists.

Eric Hoffer
American philosopher and psychologist

The illusion of knowing

Imagine a keen university student eagerly waiting for the marks for their first quiz to be released. Expectations are high as they had spent a good number of hours dedicated to studying. The weekend social activities were trimmed to a bare minimum, lectures were dutifully watched, many pages of notes taken, and anything that could be marked with a highlighting pen was painstakingly highlighted in a multitude of colours. So at exactly 9.00 am when the marks were released, nothing quite prepared them for the barely passing mark they received.

Our disappointed student is a victim of the "illusion of knowing;" a wonderful phrase that I wish I had invented. Essentially it refers to overestimating the amount that you actually know. It's closely related to the Dunning-Kruger effect, which is when people with low competence or expertise in a particular area tend to overestimate their abilities. So that's the off-key and out of tune singer competing in their local talent quest; they think they sound like Sinatra, when they sound more like Donald Duck.

#7. The trick to understanding something is knowing exactly how much you need to understand.

The illusion of knowing focuses specifically on the depth of knowledge of a particular concept or piece of information; in other words, do you know as much as you think you know. Knowledge is certainly an intriguing concept, so it should be no surprise that some of the greatest philosophers of our time have contemplated it. The Greek thinker, Plato, thought that our knowledge is innate, and that learning is really just 'recalling' information that we are born with. The British empiricists (philosophers such as John Locke, George Berkeley and David Hume) held that all knowledge comes to us through the senses. The human mind is like a blank slate (*tabula rasa*) at birth and essentially develops only through our experiences. Needless to say, there is still much debate surrounding the topic.

The fact is that knowledge is intimately linked to understanding; they are separate processes but each one depends on the other. Knowledge is about possession of information while understanding is about making sense of that information and seeing how it connects to broader concepts. So the more knowledge you have, the better chance you have of understanding something. However, the concept of 'understanding' is sometimes over-rated; naturally, it's desirable but not always essential. We know that when we put our foot on the accelerator of a car, the car will move forward. We know that putting our foot on the brake will slow the car down. But it's not really necessary for us to understand the complex engineering that makes it work (unless of course you're a mechanic).

Learners inherit the earth

The quote that opens this chapter is one plucked straight from my noticeboard, courtesy of my father. He must have read it in something he couldn't rip the page out of, because it was presented to me written neatly on lined paper. Over the years, it's been slightly reworded into different forms (like the version my father found), but the core idea is the same. The original quote is from Eric Hoffer's 1963 book *The Ordeal of Change*, "In a time of drastic change it is the learners who inherit the future. The learned usually find themselves equipped to live in a world that no longer exists."

It's tucked into a passage where Hoffer is discussing how societies (and individuals) survive and thrive during major transitions. His point is that flexibility, openness to learning, and adaptability are more valuable than just having lots of static knowledge, particularly "in times of drastic change." Learning is not a one-time event but a continuous process (as the phrase 'life-long learner' would suggest); it's fundamental to our existence as humans. It is deeply embedded in our biology, psychology, and social structures.

#8. Learning is a fundamental human skill that enables us to develop and adapt to a world that is constantly changing.

From an evolutionary perspective, the human brain has evolved to do nothing else better than learn; we are learning machines. Fundamentally, we learn in order to survive in the world, but we also learn to enrich our human experience. So the caveman learns to hunt and that enables them to get food (survival), but they still feel a sense of mastery or accomplishment by providing for their tribe (enrichment).

As you can imagine, there are many learning theories such as behaviourism, cognitivism, constructivism, and humanism, (to name but a few) and just as many theorists associated with each. These are not only taught to thousands of prospective teachers on a daily basis, but some have been embedded in education systems around the globe. Students of education and psychology would be familiar with Jean Piaget, Lev Vygotsky, Albert Bandura, Benjamin Bloom and a host of others.

Learning is a multi-faceted, multi-dimensional activity; it's a combination of our cognitive, behavioural and emotional processes. These processes are further impacted by the natural learning ability embedded in our genes along with the educational environment we have been exposed to. Understanding a little about these theories can help you become a more effective learner by understanding how different teaching methods and learning styles impact your own learning process. It also provides valuable insights into how knowledge is created and how we learn, making us equipped for future educational challenges

Why my dog will never get his PhD

It sounds harsh, but my dog Benji (a Cavoodle) will never get his PhD. However, there are many things he can do that I can't. He can smell sliced roast beef from the other side of the house, he realises someone is coming home five minutes before I do, and he remembers that there is still a treat on the bench in the carport where I left it yesterday. It really shouldn't be that surprising. Benji has a sense of smell that is 100,000 times more sensitive than that of humans, and he can hear higher and lower frequencies way better than I can.

Benji however, doesn't have a terrific sense of time. We can be away from the house for 10 minutes or 10 days; the level of excitement on our return is exactly the same. As far as I can tell, his main thought processes revolve around food and "his people" (my wife being his main person). If he had to choose between us and a box of dog treats, I think it would be a close call. It's highly unlikely Benji will be studying neuroscience – or anything else for that matter. Study is not a dog-like thing to do; but learning is.

It's lucky that Benji wasn't anywhere near the Institute of Experimental Medicine in St Petersburg, Russia, around 1900. Ivan Pavlov was a Russian physiologist who among other things studied the digestive response in dogs. By all accounts the fate (and treatment) of the now infamous Pavlovian dogs was less than optimal, however the results of his experiments revolutionised the field of psychology and changed the way we understood learning.

Pavlov noticed that his dogs started to salivate as they saw the white lab coats of the assistants who fed them. The key point was that the dogs didn't need to see or taste the food in order to react physically. This is unusual, as physiologically speaking, dogs should only salivate when presented with food (not white lab coats). It's an unconditioned (or more correctly "unconditional") reflex. The connection of the white lab coat to the food holds the key. Over time the dogs had associated the sight of the lab coats with food – hence, salivation. Pavlov started to experiment with other stimuli using everything from buzzers to metronomes to successfully elicit salivation. As an interesting aside, it seems Pavlov never actually used a bell, as the literature would suggest.

Benji running to the door and barking as soon as he hears keys jingling is classical conditioning. He has (quite rightly) associated the jingling keys with his people leaving. It is a learned behaviour. It's the same reason we may associate a certain smell, a song, or a movie, with a person or a specific memory. So, how does a salivating dog relate to your life as a student?

To give just a few examples: studying in a regular place helps reinforce the connection between that place (perhaps your desk or a library), and the act of concentrating on a task. The importance of a workplace is exactly as the name suggests; it is a *place* where you regularly go to *work*. One of the difficulties of working from home is that 'home' is a place where traditionally you would *not* be working. That's why students are advised not to study in front of the television (a place of entertainment), or even worse, in bed (a place of sleep). Studying at the same time regularly also forms and association between that time of day, and study. Every day I try to work on my writing projects between 8.30 am and 10.30 am, and then 5.30 pm to 7.30 pm. When I go to our regular café, I usually take my laptop; so now I associate the café more with writing than I do with coffee – classical conditioning in action.

Bobo and beyond

Apart from conditioning, much of our own learning is done through 'modelling' and problem-solving. Modelling (also known as observational or social learning) is the process of learning by copying others' behaviour. Thanks to a round-bottomed toy, psychologist Albert Bandura conducted a series of experiments in the early 1960s that elegantly showed just how pervasive observational learning is. The toy is inflatable, with water or sand at the bottom. If you hit it, it will wobble for a few moments and eventually bobble back to an upright position. I actually owned one of these and I remember it being fun and infuriating all at the same time.

Bandura's famous *Bobo Doll Study* used two groups of children; the first group was shown a video of a woman hitting and yelling at the doll, while the other group was not shown the video. When given their own Bobo doll to play with, many of children from the first group also hit and yelled at the doll; none of the children from the other group did. Students can learn effective study techniques by observing their peers, teachers, parents, or anyone who they look up to. When I was a student, I remember making hundreds of flashcards after seeing them used successfully by one of my classmates.

Observational learning, however, can go beyond simply copying behaviours. If we are given enough cues, we can also learn how to think. A maths teacher, for example, can 'think aloud', commenting on each step while solving problems, enabling students to internalise the reasoning process. Traditionally, in an apprenticeship the novice learns skills by observing and practicing under a master. The term 'cognitive apprenticeship framework' describes this approach which is designed to help students learn by making thinking processes visible and explicit. This type of observational learning is an excellent example of teaching 'what' was done to solve a particular problem, and also teaching the 'how and 'why'.

So much of what I do now reflects the behaviours I observed in my parents. I watched my father carefully organise all of this things – I do the same. I would watch my mother engage in friendly banter with virtually everyone she meets – this is something I do. I was raised in a household where education and scholarship were very highly valued. Of course, I eventually had a career in education. All three of my children chose to attend university, even though the option not to was always available. Observational learning is a powerful tool for any student to utilise because it leverages the innate human ability to learn by watching others.

Humuhumunukunukuapua'a

When I 'get into something', I'm all in: typewriters, pens, cameras, coins and banknotes, astronomy, backgammon, chess; that's just the tip of the iceberg. My enthusiasm for each of these endeavours waxes and wanes like the tide. I will enthusiastically trawl the internet for any available information, buy books, join forums, find newsletters, browse catalogues, in other words, completely immerse myself in the world of Montblanc fountain pens (for example). I could tell you all about the countless nib variations, the most desirable pen to own, and what the differences are between a Montblanc 144, 147 and 149. Then in a blink of an eye, I don't use, look at, or even think about a single pen for months. I'm probably no different to the thousands of enthusiasts for almost any hobby sport or pastime.

My oldest daughter, Gabi, can recite the lyrics (complete with accompanying dance moves) to the movies, *High School Musical I, II* and *III*. It's remarkable (and highly entertaining) to watch. She can re-enact entire scenes word-for-word without missing a beat. She could also tell you that "Humuhumunukunukuapua'a" is the eleventh song on the *High School Musical 2* soundtrack, and then proceed to sing it flawlessly. *[Fun fact: the humuhumunukunukuapua'a is actually the state fish of Hawaii, the reef triggerfish.]*

When I asked her how she managed to achieve such an amazing intellectual feat, she looked at me strangely, wondering what 'intellectual feat' I was talking about. Well … learning. Learning all the lyrics, dialogue, dance moves, and remembering it all. Her response was, "It didn't really feel like learning; I just love High School Musical." And that is the key point. I could probably ask the same question at any Comic-Con or similar pop-culture event and the responses would most likely be identical. Fans were motivated to learn as much as they could about their favourite show, for example, because they were interested … and they stayed interested because they were motivated.

Motivation is one of the key forces that drive human behaviour. As you might expect, there are many well known motivational theories (Maslow's hierarchy of needs, for example), but in the context of study, it would be difficult to avoid Ryan and Deci's Self-Determination Theory. This is a psychological framework developed by Edward Deci and Richard Ryan in the mid 1980s, which focuses on human motivation, well-being, and personal growth. It distinguishes between intrinsic and extrinsic motivation. Intrinsic motivation is the drive to engage in an activity for its own sake, because it is inherently interesting, enjoyable, or satisfying. Extrinsic motivation is the drive to perform an activity to achieve an external reward or avoid punishment, for example studying to get a good grade or avoid failing.

Intrinsic motivation leads to better understanding and retention. It intuitively makes sense – you learn better when you're interested in what you are learning. The focus is on the activity itself rather than the outcome. Of course, the two types of motivation are not mutually exclusive. In most cases both intrinsic and extrinsic motivation will drive you to do well.

There are plenty of studies that show that students with high motivation tend to exert more effort, persist longer, and achieve better academic outcomes. As a student, your motivation and interest drives the effort and persistence needed to acquire knowledge, while interest creates engagement which in turn makes learning more meaningful.

6. INFORMATION OVERLOAD

"It's not information overload. It's filter failure."

Clay Shirky
American writer, educator, and technology theorist

Defining existence

Quite some time ago two large, heavy boxes arrived at my home, shipped all the way from Western Australia; they contained something I had wanted for a long time. Thanks to eBay and a seller keen to downsize, I now owned the 20 volume set of the *Oxford English Dictionary*. Just to be clear, that's not 20 dictionaries; that's *one* dictionary in 20 volumes. It takes up 1.2 metres of shelf space and weighs about 70 kilos. It's perhaps the greatest single reference work ever published. I love owning it, but to be honest, I'm far more likely to refer to the same dictionary I have been using for the better part of 50 years: *The Concise Oxford Dictionary (5th edition)* printed in 1965. My battered old copy is a hardcover version about the size of a brick. It's the one book that sits permanently on my desk.

Every student should own a hard copy dictionary. Whether it's brand new or second-hand, trust me, it won't cost very much, but the investment is well worth it. It doesn't really matter what dictionary you buy; choose one you like. I know what you're thinking: why would you buy a heavy printed dictionary when we can just go online. The online process is, one 'click' and you're there – instant definition in a nanosecond, and most of the time that's a perfect outcome. But the process of hunting down a word in a physical hardcopy book involves being exposed to many other new words. I often notice unexplored words above, below and near the entry I'm looking for. For me, that's the best part … it's an adventure.

#9. Your life as a student will be ruled by the quality and quantity of words you use; the dictionary should become your new best friend.

In everyday life no one ever thinks about a word count (imagine if we did), but as a student every essay and report is defined by it. Marks are deducted if you go under or exceed the given word limit (usually plus or minus 10%). The number of words you are expected to produce somehow has a mysterious way of increasing the more you study. If you are a first year university student, then 1000 word essays are the norm; by the third year it's 3000 words. The average honours thesis is between 10,000 to 15,000 words while a doctoral dissertation can be up to 100,000 words. But of course, it's not just about the quantity of words; the *quality* of words we use enables us, as humans, to communicate and express our ideas, thoughts and emotions. Words represent the building blocks of our spoken language, and it's through language that we categorise, name, and interpret all the things around us.

In the late 1980s, chief editor of the Oxford English Dictionary (OED), John Simpson, asked the poet Benjamin Zephaniah about the origins of the noun "skanking". Zephaniah decided that the only way to explain was to come to the OED office in person and demonstrate. 'Skanking' was included in the dictionary with the following definition: "a style of West Indian dancing to reggae music, in which the body bends forward at the waist, and the knees are raised and the hands claw the air in time to the beat".

Without words, it would be difficult to describe the world, our emotions, or even our own identities. Words allow us to explain what we experience, and help us shape how we interpret those experiences. They turn the intangible into something we can share and understand collectively. So words don't just describe existence, they give it form, meaning, and depth.

The 5000 ton book

Nine-year-old Milton Sirotta probably had no idea that a simple word he made up in 1920 would become one of the most valuable brands in existence. Sirotta's uncle, mathematician Edward Kasner, used the word 'googol' in his book *Mathematics and the Imagination*. It was used to describe the concept of a very large number, and 'very large' in this case is larger than the number of atoms in the observable universe.

For someone of my generation, the fact that Google was founded in 1998 is close to mind-bending. In the world of information technology, that is a lifetime ago, but in real terms, it's not long at all. Larry Page and Sergey Brin created what is now probably the most used search engine in the world while they were PhD students at Stanford University; it was initially a research project designed to improve how search engines indexed and ranked web pages. They wanted a catchy name that reflected the massive amount of information they aimed to organise. They chose Googol, which morphed into Google; whether it's a derivative or was simply misspelled is still debated. Either way, the word has found its way into everyday language, with the verb "google" added to the *Oxford English Dictionary* in 2006.

I grew up in an era when all we ever needed was a fairly small drop of information, and that information was usually directly relevant to our lives – the weather forecast, sports results, and the evening news. To a large extent, that was all technology ever allowed us to access. In Australia, there were only four television channels to choose from and all programming would stop at midnight. The station would remain off the air until the mid morning. The nightly news was at 7.00 pm and lasted 30 minutes. Newsreaders sat at their desk and read the news, with only the most major of world events travelling beyond international borders. Of course, it was all in black and white. Phones were rotary dial, no one other than NASA owned a computer, and we all wrote by hand or on a typewriter.

In my first year of university (we're going back to 1980) the library still had a card catalogue, and finding a journal article meant physically locating it on the library shelves. If it was a popular reference book, you probably wouldn't even find it as students would sometimes hide them so they could access it the next morning. If you were lucky enough to find what you were after, you either had to make handwritten notes there and then, or carry the large volume down to the usually crowded photocopy room armed with a pocketful of coins, then wait for hours in a queue to laboriously photocopy each page.

The growth of the Internet heralded massive changes, particularly in the way we navigated our way through the maze of available resources. We used a mysterious thing called a 'search engine' with the most popular one at the time having quite a funny name – Yahoo. In my great big list of "books I should have kept" is one called *The Internet yellow pages*. It was a 700 page soft cover book which essentially listed thousands of websites in alphabetical order, organised by categories like science, business, and entertainment. The book was about 5 centimetres thick and weighed about 1.5 kilograms. I find it amusing to ponder that if printed today, a similar directory would be 100 kilometres thick and weigh over 5,000 tons!

There is no denying that the Internet is an amazing resource. It provides instant access to a vast amount of information from around the world. It's easy to use, constantly updated, and allows users to find answers, resources, and expert opinions on almost any topic.

Why I love Wikipedia

I remember when my parents purchased our *World Book* encyclopedia; it was an expensive purchase at the time. I'm so glad we still have that original set. In the mid 1970's the average wage in Australia was $7,600 and my parents paid around $375 dollars for the encyclopedia – so a little over two and a half weeks wages. However, it was not as expensive as the *Encyclopedia Britannica* which was considered the gold standard, and was close to double the cost. This represented a significant investment for families, but parents were keen to give their children the best possible advantage when in came to education.

Unlike the *Britannica*, *The World Book* was generally considered to be more accessible and entertaining with its colour pictures and lots of illustrations. Michael Vincent O'Shea, a professor of education at the University of Wisconsin became the founding editor in 1917. He felt that a "common defect" of encyclopedias was that they were too "formal and technical," something he wanted to avoid with *The World Book*. It was quite a revolutionary approach for that era. His observation echoes some of the themes of this book – education and learning need not always be formal and technical.

Like many printed books, the information contained in encyclopedias quickly becomes outdated. To mitigate this, the editors would release yearly updates in the form of the *Year Book*. My father bought me these for a good 20 years after we purchased the original edition. While they provided excellent snapshots of information relevant to a particular year, there was no efficient way of cross-referencing back to the main volumes. Wouldn't it be great if we could have an encyclopedia with real-time updates and no need for any Year Books. In fact, imagine if you could edit the encyclopedia itself, under the watchful eye of a world wide community who are quick to correct any glaring errors. But that's not all; with magical things called hyperlinks you get a near superhuman power to instantly jump to another piece of information. Imagine that.

Welcome to Wikipedia. Launched in 2001 by Jimmy Wales and Larry Sanger, Wikipedia is an online encyclopedia created and maintained by a community of volunteer editors using a wiki-based editing system; one that allows users to create, edit, and organise content directly within a web browser ("wiki" is Hawaiian for "quick"). I'm a big fan. It's the only place where I can learn about quantum mechanics, ancient history, and cryptography, and then get an episode-by-episode breakdown of the sitcom *Seinfeld*, all in one sitting. I've often lost myself in hours of research, leap-frogging from topic to topic so many times I'd completely forgotten where I started from.

Even though Wikipedia is currently the largest and most popular general reference work on the World Wide Web, it's generally frowned upon in the academic community. The criticisms are mainly centred on the site's collaborative nature, and that the information may not be reliable given that anyone can edit and create content. Critics suggest the site can exhibit bias and be prone to manipulation particularly when it comes to controversial topics. However this is a criticism that could easily be (and often is) levelled at any of the prestigious peer-reviewed academic journals. The fact remains that Wikipedia is unparalleled in its scope and currency of information. If a celebrity is involved in any incident, Wikipedia will reflect this often within minutes. This immediacy is something even the best journals simply cannot achieve. I find Wikipedia incredibly useful, as long as I follow-up on the sources it references. My philosophy in this regard is best summed up by the adage: Wikipedia is like a sausage; it's best not to know how it's made.

Choice, complexity, chaos

There was a point in history when getting any information at all was a challenge. Like one drop of water at a time, knowledge, stories, and culture were passed down through the spoken word and cave paintings. Early writing systems expanded our ability to communicate, and the use of paper revolutionised the process of documentation; now we could keep and store information to pass on and share with others. But it was generally a small number of others, and a relatively small amount of information. More drops, a bit more water. The invention of the Gutenberg printing press in the mid 15th century made books accessible to the masses so now more people could access more information. More water for everyone.

Fast forward to an era where a massive amount of information can be accessed in a blink of an eye, by more people than ever before, on a something as small as an iPhone. And all this can be done at any time, and anywhere in the world. Information rushes at us in countless formats, and we're drawn towards it like moths to the flame. Content has become currency - everything from pioneering academic reports to the latest musings of friends in our social networks. The floodgates have opened.

Okay, so there's a lot of information - but how do we process it all? The answer is: we don't. When the amount of input to a system is greater than its processing capacity a reduction in 'decision quality' will occur. That's the idea behind "information overload," a term coined in 1964 by Bertram Gross, Professor of Political Science at Hunter College. The concept gained widespread attention and became better-known through Alvin Toffler's book *Future Shock*. Toffler expanded on Gross's ideas, describing the overwhelming effects of rapid technological change and the increasing volume of information that individuals and society would have to deal with.

Of course, not everyone feels overwhelmed by the torrent of information. Some are addicted to it; checking their iPhone first thing in the morning, then trawling though volumes of promotional material, emails, news feeds and social media updates. The challenge no longer lies in simply getting information, but in knowing what to do with it.

Filtering out the noise, and prioritising quality over quantity, allows you to focus on what truly matters. Put simply you need to know what *not* to know. The concept has been discussed in various forms throughout history, however was given a formal structure by German sociologist and economist Ralph Hertwig and his colleagues in their 2016 book *Deliberate Ignorance: Choosing Not to Know*. The notion of "deliberate ignorance" is the decision to avoid or reject certain types of knowledge or information, even when it is available.

> *#10. The world has become a chaotic place,*
> *and the internet only amplifies the noise.*
> *Finding clarity in the chaos is a superpower.*

In the aftermath of the 2005 London Underground bombings, the news coverage was incessant and the images were distressing. The commentary repeated the same thing over and over, which served no purpose other than to sensationalise a tragic situation. I decided there and then to stop watching or listening to any news – on television, radio, newspapers and online. This is something I still do to this day. I replaced news with music, art and literature, which to me was far more rewarding and uplifting. I was shocked at how my perception of the world changed for the better – immediately. If there is a major news event that I really feel I should be aware of, I would carefully sift through the various news sources that I'm comfortable with.

The term 'mindful consumption' is usually used in the context of sustainability and being a responsible consumer. It is simply, the practice of being aware of our choices when it comes to what we consume. The mindful consumption of media has served me well for decades. It's also a concept that translates well to the consumption of information in general. Set limits, be selective, and be aware. That's an excellent way to wade through the complexity and chaos of information overload.

HAL 9000

In 1968 MGM released *2001: A Space Odyssey*. In the movie, a computer named HAL (the HAL 9000) was designed to control the systems of the Discovery One spacecraft and assist the astronauts with their mission to Jupiter. The computer's primary role was to ensure the success of the mission, but ultimately Hal goes rogue.

Given the script was written in the 1960's, HAL is a very good approximation of artificial intelligence as we know it now. Artificial Intelligence (AI) refers to the simulation of human intelligence processes by machines, particularly computer systems. One such system is

ChatGPT, an advanced language model developed by OpenAI. It is designed to understand and generate human-like text based on the input it receives. Unlike HAL 9000, ChatGPT isn't exactly a "computer," but rather a software program that *runs* on computers. It can perform a wide range of tasks, from answering questions to engaging in detailed conversations, providing explanations, and even helping with tasks like creative writing, or research.

Fortunately, ChatGPT can't go rogue (or at least, we hope not!). But like all AI systems, it has important limitations. Artificial intelligence relies heavily on the data it has been trained on (in the same way humans learn from experience and exposure). However, if that data is incomplete, biased, or skewed in some way, the AI's outputs will inevitably reflect those flaws. This is not true intelligence in the human sense; it's a sophisticated simulation. It's *artificial*.

AI doesn't understand the world – it processes patterns. It lacks awareness, consciousness, and the capacity to comprehend meaning in the way humans do. It can't grasp abstract concepts, pick up on emotional nuance, or read between the lines. It has no intuition, no sense of context beyond what patterns suggest, and no lived experience to draw from.

Humans, by contrast, make intuitive leaps, interpret metaphors, detect irony, and generate insight based on a rich and complex understanding of the world. We connect ideas in ways that defy algorithms. That's what makes human intelligence not just functional, but creative, empathetic, and profound. These are things artificial intelligence, no matter how advanced, still cannot truly replicate.

Still ... what it *can* do is both amazing and frightening. The following is 'conversation' I had with ChatGPT, while writing this section. Not a single word has been altered.

Me: Hi ChatGPT, how are you?

ChatGPT: Hi! I'm doing well, thanks for asking. How about you?

Me: Really good. I'm working on a book for students at the moment.

ChatGPT: That's fantastic! What's the book about? I'd love to help if you need any input or ideas.

Me: It's designed to shift the focus away from the anxiety related to study, towards the personal rewards that study can bring.

ChatGPT: That sounds like an incredibly valuable approach, especially for students who often feel overwhelmed by academic pressure. Focusing on the personal growth and rewards of learning can make studying more enjoyable and fulfilling. How are you planning to convey this message in the book? Will it be through personal stories, practical tips, or something else?

Me: I'm so glad you asked. I'm using a combination of exactly what you just mentioned: personal stories, practical tips, and hopefully using 35 years of experience and wisdom gained as an educator.

ChatGPT: That sounds like a powerful mix! Your experience as an educator will definitely add depth and credibility to your insights. Personal stories can make the content relatable, while practical tips can provide students with actionable strategies. Do you have any specific themes or chapters planned out yet? Or any particular stories you're excited to include?

Me: The book is called "How to be a rotten student: A personal manifesto." There chapters on how to get started, keep things simple, avoid procrastination, perfectionism ... and even a chapter on how to *stop* studying.

ChatGPT: I love the title—it's catchy and intriguing! The chapters you've outlined sound both practical and relatable. Approaching common student challenges like procrastination and perfectionism with a fresh perspective can really resonate with readers.

Our conversation continued like this in a disarmingly 'human' fashion. I thanked my AI friend for the conversation and mentioned "I better get back to work."

ChatGPT: I'm glad to hear that! It sounds like you're making great progress with your book. If you ever need more ideas or support, feel free to reach out. Good luck, and happy writing! :-)

I was amazed and a bit overwhelmed all at the same time. That's one of the defining features of AI, it almost seems like I'm talking to a real person. Still, no matter how we look at it, AI is an incredible tool which is changing the landscape not only of education, but most fields of human endeavour. AI wasn't available when I first started writing this book, but for the last few drafts I used it extensively when researching dates, and events, and in clarifying concepts often difficult to grasp. It has saved me literally hundreds of hours of research.

7. THE STUDENT MINDSET

> The first step towards getting somewhere is to decide that you are not going to stay where you are.
>
> *Chauncey Depew*
> *US Senator (in office 1899-1911)*

Welcome to the Frisbee club

Some days are so good you could just bottle them and keep them forever. Today was one of those days. I had my regular swim at the Macquarie University pool, and decided to walk to the campus 'quadrangle' to get arguably the world's best Korean ramen. It was orientation week; O-Week for short. The sun was shining and the campus was bustling with activity. There were lots of stands set up for various campus clubs and societies, with loyal members eager to snare some new recruits. It was the usual collection of sporty (and quite a few not-so-sporty) groups: the swimming club, squash, football, drama, chess club (naturally), and my favourite, the Ultimate Frisbee club.

It bought back so many lovely memories of my orientation week on the same campus over 40 years go. In terms of the atmosphere, virtually nothing has changed. Students wandered around, wide-eyed and optimistic; some on their own, some with friends, and a few desperately trying to distance themselves from their hovering parents. The clothes were casual but carefully selected. I still remember the immense sense of freedom. My high school canteen gave way to a plethora of food halls, cafes and even a uni bar. This was no longer compulsory education. I was in the real world now, studying what I wanted to study. Lectures were highly encouraged, but optional. Given the number of extracurricular activities on offer, I suspect even study itself was highly encouraged, but optional.

I sat happily eating my Ramen watching the Ultimate Frisbee Club members showing interested onlookers how to throw and catch the Frisbee. They made it look easy. I'm not quite sure why, but to me, throwing a Frisbee around is such a quintessentially 'college' thing to do. It must have something to do with the hundreds of American movies I'd seen depicting college life. If the Frisbee club was around back when I started, I would have joined for sure.

It's important to engage not only with the academic side of your institution but also with its social and cultural life. Get involved, stay active, and connect with others. Forming meaningful relationships can make your educational journey more enjoyable and fulfilling. These connections often provide both academic and emotional support when you need it most, and can become a lasting part of your personal and professional life well beyond your years of study.

For most students, orientation week is the first step in their education journey. There are many quotes that incorporate the notion of making a start. One I really like is courtesy of Chauncey Depew, a US Senator in office at the turn of the 20th century: "The first step towards getting somewhere is to decide that you are not going to stay where you are." It appeals to me because it's not always about the end goal, as motivational experts would have you believe. It's sometimes simply about not wanting to be where you currently are.

Failing the fun run

There is nothing fun about a 'fun run' ... at least not the one's I've been in. You embrace the event with all the naïve enthusiasm of a chicken not realising that it is eventually destined for dinner. Before the race, I would picture myself in the elite leading pack, powering ahead with gazelle-like strides with the image of great Olympians foremost on my mind. It's just under 14 kilometres ... I mean, how hard can it be?

CUT TO SMALL CROWD GATHERED AROUND AN EXHAUSTED RUNNER. HE IS SITTING ON THE ROAD, HEAD IN HANDS.

          PERSON IN CROWD
I think we need medical ...

          RUNNER
(COMPLETELY OUT OF BREATH)
No, no ... I'm good.

          PERSON
(MOTIONING FOR FIRST AID)
You don't look too good ...

          RUNNER
(OUT OF BREATH) I'm fine ...
(ANOTHER HUGE BREATH)
I'm really fine ... just need a minute.

          PERSON
Have you had anything to drink?

          RUNNER
Yeah ... I had some tea this morning.

          ANOTHER PERSON
Did you do any training for this?

          RUNNER
(STILL OUT OF BREATH)
... used to run at school.

          PERSON
What's with the shoes?

RUNNER STANDS – SHAKEY.

RUNNER

... they're comfortable.

YET ANOTHER PERSON

They're not even running shoes!

The scenario may seem exaggerated, but I did exactly this many years ago in an ill-fated fun run; no water, wrong shoes, no training – only a blind optimism that somehow I'll get to the end. I did get to the end, but not without some serious damage to my feet (blisters) and my ego. I ran the same race the following year with far more preparation and far more success.

I'm sure you get the point of the story. It doesn't matter whether you are at school, university or college – there is a lot you can do before the semester even starts. My youngest daughter Emily, would spend hours (if not days) planning the intricate stationery requirements for each of her units, getting the perfect folders, pens, notepads, along with Post-It notes ... usually colour coordinated according to some arcane system. While it certainly amuses me, it is an important step in her pre-semester process. I was no different. At the start of every school year one of the best bits was getting the new textbooks and buying all the stationery.

Preparation for study means having everything you need organised and ready; things like a computer and somewhere to work (even if that's a library). If there is an orientation session, make sure you attend (I can't stress how import that is). Read your unit guides, browse through your textbook, and work out how to log on to your learning platform. Familiarise yourself with your class timetable and mark important dates (assessment deadlines, exams) in a planner or digital calendar. Try to establish a routine that includes your work, social activities and some sort of sport or exercise.

There is so much information available on this kind of thing that I almost feel silly writing about it. The bottom line is, do as much as you can before your first class, because it will make your semester a great deal easier (think hydration, proper shoes and some pre-race training).

How to become a zombie

There is nothing quite like watching the sun go down, working all night, infusing yourself with copious amounts of coffee, watching the sun come up, and then in the last minute, handing in an *almost* acceptable assessment. It's a unique form of student torture. By midnight you start to feel tired, but fear not, that's what the third coffee is for. Your eyes are itchy and bloodshot, but they still function, which is more than can be said for your brain, which has rapidly begun to shut down. By 4.00 am, you're so light-headed with fatigue and hunger that you can hardly read the words you've already written, let alone think of new ones. By 6.00 am, you're barely conscious, but when you read your work back it *almost* makes some kind of perverse sense. You literally feel like a zombie for the rest of the day, but at least the assignment is done.

The infamous 'all-nighter' is almost a right-of-passage in the life of a student; I had quite a few in my undergraduate years. I still have the small stove top single cup Bialetti coffee percolator that accompanied me on these disastrous evenings. About 20% of college students report forgoing sleep at least once a month in order to complete an assignment at least once a month, while 35% frequently stay up past 3 a.m.

For many students, scrambling to complete an assessment in the absolute last minute can be a result of bad time management. Most students are notorious in underestimating the time they need to study, and overestimating how much they can get done. Almost all books on study (and self-help books on pretty much everything else) usually have some sort of advice on time management. That makes sense, because time is an important concept. Everything we do either sits within it, or depends on it – including study. My take on this topic was developed while I was part of a small independent theatre company. My primary responsibility was to write the plays, but quite often I was also the producer. A successful production was one where we didn't lose any money; a *very* successful production meant we actually made money, and could pay the actors.

'Manny's Law' (if I can call it that) was: "Estimate how much everything will cost, then double it; estimate how much we might make, then halve it." Funnily enough, that's usually exactly what happened and most of our productions came in almost perfectly on budget. It's a good point to consider when completing any assessment plans.

#11. When planning anything, the only thing you can expect is that it will take more time than you expected.

Assessments will almost always take longer than anticipated. The time you thought you had to complete that 2000 word essay can evaporate in a blink of an eye. It could be an unexpected visit, an unplanned social engagement, or a niggling task that simply couldn't wait ... you get the idea. The extra planning is well worth the effort; perhaps you can avoid becoming a zombie when assessments are due.

Don't be scared of change

One thing you will definitely encounter in your life as a student is change: moving from one grade to another, transitioning between schools, or shifting from classroom to online learning. Your lecturers will change; your timetables will change, as will your classrooms. Every semester will herald a change of units. You may even change where you are studying, and what you are studying. The units you might have expected to find interesting may turn out not to be, and the ones you were dreading can end up as the favourite.

Adapting to change is essential, both during your studies and throughout life, because the world is in constant motion. Today's workplaces are fast-paced and ever-evolving, with industries, roles, and technologies shifting rapidly. Those who embrace adaptability are better positioned to pursue lifelong learning and seize new opportunities as they arise. While sometimes change can feel unsettling, learning to navigate new environments, ideas, and people expands your perspective and builds resilience. The key is to view change not as a threat, but as a chance to grow, explore, and evolve.

For many students, embarking on study itself is a big change; particularly if they have been in the workforce, have travelled, raised families, or done all three. Adapting to student life after a long (or even short) break comes with its own unique personal and academic challenges. Students may feel out of practice with academic skills such as writing essays and conducting research; the advances in educational technology may feel intimidating for those who haven't studied in years. The good news is that the technology is often your best friend when it comes to assimilating back into the world of study. There are so many online resources to choose from. Larger institutions will have support services, workshops and courses for study skills, academic writing, or specific subject areas.

Another very common focus for student angst is uncertainty about a particular course of study. Questions like "Have I done the right thing?", "Is this the right qualification?", or "Have I chosen the right path?" often loom large, especially in the early stages of a program. My thinking on this subject is:

> *#12. It's the right path until you figure out that it's the wrong one.*

It's quite common for students to change their fields of interest many times during their studies. I started out studying psychology, and then briefly (and disastrously) switched to accounting and finance. After a break of a few years I switched to English literature, and finally landed with a bachelor's degree majoring in mass communication and philosophy. Don't be scared to change. There is not much point to achieving a goal you never wanted in the first place.

My Pulitzer Prize

I've lost count of how many awards I've won. I've written several best-sellers, have been interviewed by Oprah, all while maintaining a busy touring schedule drumming for a mega-band at most of the world's biggest rock stadiums. Daydreaming? Yes, of course; and just like so many aspiring young musicians, wooden spoons became drumsticks and Mum's old Slazenger tennis racket morphed into the perfect air guitar. As a 14 year old, a few days filming with a Canon Super 8 camera and I was Steven Spielberg.

Pretending to be a drummer or a Hollywood filmmaker somehow began to make the concept real. I purchased an old drum kit, and like so many teenagers formed a garage band. I upgraded my Super 8 camera to a more sophisticated one. Our films became a little more ambitious. Eventually, I really did end up playing in a rock band, and I did work professionally in the film industry.

A lot has been written about the mind's power to influence behaviour. Napoleon Hill's 1937 classic, *Think and Grow Rich* sold 15 million copies. In the early 2000's Rhonda Byrne caused a sensation with her book, *The Secret*. These books (and countless others) essentially extol the virtue of 'manifesting'. The phenomenon is certainly not new. American sociologist, Robert K. Merton coined the term 'self-fulfilling prophecy' in

1948. It refers to a prediction that may come true mainly because of a person's belief or expectation that it will. To me, the implications of this effect, both positive and negative, are profound.

Students will often announce that, "I always fail exams," or that they hate a particular subject, or that they're just not good at maths. It's an endless list. A poor performance will only reinforce what you thought to be true in the first place ("See, I told you I'm not good at maths"). There are literally dozens of variations of essentially the same theme: the observer-expectancy effect, the placebo effect, feedback loops, the Pygmalion effect, and of course, 'manifesting'. Ultimately, it doesn't matter what you call it, the trick is to reverse the process and harness the self-fulfilling prophecy to your advantage.

Visualise yourself finishing school successfully, or being awarded the diploma or degree. The more vivid the 'daydream' the better it is. It reinforces belief in your ability and motivates you to act. Manifesting isn't just about positive thinking; it also requires taking *actionable* steps towards your goal. Now, if you'll excuse me. I'm off to collect my Pulitzer Prize.

8. DO LESS ... SIMPLIFY

Any fool can make something complicated.
It is hard to make something simple.

Sir Richard Branson
English business person

Less is more

As an aspiring drummer, my first venture into a real studio was to record a 'demo tape' for our band. The producer, Mal Green, had been the drummer in a very well known 1980s band, Split Enz. I was a big fan. Not only was I using his drum kit, but I was playing under the watchful eye of one of my favourite drummers. I had a habit of punctuating virtually every bar with a resounding crash on the aptly named crash cymbal. It was fun to do, but clouded the recording by producing a sea of reverberating noise throughout the whole song. At the end of the track, Mal came up to me and said (very diplomatically), "Try it again Manny, but this time imagine you're only allowed to use your crash cymbal once. Less is more." The track sounded *way* better.

Now the cynic in me rolls his eyes. Come on people, how can less be more? It's either less, or it's more, right? I mean, technically this little aphorism doesn't even make sense, but the philosophy behind it most definitely does. Sometimes you really can achieve more, by doing less. The phrase first appeared in a Robert Browning poem (*Andrea del Sarto*) in the mid 1800's, but was catapulted to notoriety by the design movement in the 20th century. It became the dictum of everything from art and literature to living a minimalist lifestyle.

It's an important maxim on so many levels when it comes to study. There are times when the best decision a student can make is to cut a unit, or even a few units. It's better to pass everything you attempt, than to fail a unit because you have simply taken on too much work. But even when it comes to how much you study, the "less is more" principle applies. Study less. Teachers will usually tell you to study more. That seems to be the number one solution for almost everything, "You just need to study more." What is the point of having a terrific study strategy if it takes over 5 hours every night – you may get excellent grades ... but at what cost?

Studying just to rack up the hours is pointless. Your aim should be to study the *least* amount of time to achieve the *best* possible results. This means studying more efficiently, or to use a well worn phrase: "work smarter; not harder." There are literally thousands of websites and books that will help a great deal. I can shamelessly recommend my own book *Study Right*, as a good "how to study" guide. But whichever resource you use, it will only be useful if you actively apply the suggestions given.

The key to studying less and getting more done is to use 'active learning strategies'. Simply reading the same thing over and over again, will work ... to an extent. You become very familiar with the material, but familiarity is not the same as understanding. It's easy to overestimate how well you know something (remember, "the illusion of knowing"). It's way better to regularly test yourself on what you've read. You could make flash cards or use any of the excellent apps that are available. Try to make connections between the things you've just learned and the things you already know. The term educators love to use is 'scaffolding'. It's an appropriate term as essentially you are trying to build on the foundation of knowledge you have already accumulated.

Instead of passively rereading or highlighting vast slabs of text, which can feel productive but often wastes time, active learning forces your brain to engage with what you're studying, improving retention and understanding. As a result, you spend less time relearning information later on and can focus your efforts more precisely, reducing the total hours needed to master a subject. Simple.

Don't read your textbook

In the late 1950s and early 1960s American educator, Evelyn Wood developed a 'speed reading' method she called Reading Dynamics. It essentially involved techniques such as minimising subvocalisation (that little voice in your head that reads along), using peripheral vision to take in more words at once, and skimming for key ideas instead of reading every single word. Speed reading became something of a 'craze', thanks to clever marketing and a few high profile endorsements. Its popularity makes perfect sense, as people in business, government, and education were constantly looking for ways to absorb information faster.

My father, always keen to further my education, sent me to a week long speed reading course in the mid 1970s. Did it work? Short answer: kind of, but not like the hype suggests. To understand complex material and *really* retain information, our brain needs time to process meaning, not just words. Nevertheless, speed reading can certainly help you move through pages faster, which is often precisely the idea when faced with a mountain of journal articles or textbooks to wade through.

When we think of 'reading', it normally means taking each word one at a time, and progressing through a book, page by page, chapter by chapter. However, there are different types of 'reading': reading for pleasure, skimming, scanning, or careful and deliberate reading to understand something. Textbooks or journal articles are not novels. That may seem obvious, but many students still treat them as if they were.

#13. The only person who should be reading a textbook word for word, is the person who wrote it.

The best way to start any form of research is to use what I call the "smorgasbord strategy." Start with an overview and once you have the big picture, select the various texts, journals and chapters to review in greater detail. The summary of an academic journal article is contained in the Abstract at the start. If the source looks promising, you can read the introduction and conclusion to get more detail. With a textbook, simply scanning the back cover is a good start. Then have a look at the preface, which is where the author will usually preview each chapter. The body of any textbook is generally highly organised; each chapter may have a neatly placed summary or outline at the start or end. If not, then the first paragraph of the chapter will usually preview what will follow.

If your textbook has any review questions at the end of each chapter, it's definitely worth looking at these, especially if you are sitting an exam on the subject. They may give valuable clues to the type of questions which might be asked. It's not exactly speed reading, but it's very close.

A guide to cramming

Cramming is working intensively to absorb large volumes of information in a short amount of time. The prevailing wisdom is that it is to be avoided. The brain can only process a small number of facts or thoughts at any one given time, so cramming doesn't give the brain enough time to synthesise the information and find connections. It's also less useful when it comes to understanding, comprehension and application – it's mainly just utilising memory. But let's face it; cramming also has a quite a few benefits. The logic is that it's still better to do work in the last minute than to do nothing at all.

When it comes to assessments and essays, students have a few options such as requesting an extension or simply accepting a late-penalty. However, exams are far more brutal with a definitive and immovable deadline. Yet, even so, many students will be overcome by a strange sense of optimism … "I'll be okay," they think, "I'll wing it." Panic doesn't set in until the night before.

So, with exams in mind, there are a few different levels of cramming: the night before cram, the last minute cram, and absolute last second cram. The 'absolute last second' cram is as frantic as it sounds. Here you are virtually praying for a miracle; hoping that against all odds, you might just somehow scrape through a unit that has all but flat-lined. In the case of an exam, it's a last-ditch effort to perhaps kick start a few dormant synapses into delivering a correct answer. In this instance, it is vital you have selected the most relevant information. You are essentially relying on short-term memory to recall information that you scanned a few minutes before walking into the exam room.

The "last-minute cram" is a little more forgiving, but not much. Most educators would say you are adding extra stress to an already stressful situation and that it's ineffective. My take on it is that *not* cramming is even more ineffective, as you are doing nothing. There is a lot of information that you can assimilate and it may make the difference between a pass and a fail.

The "night-before cram" is more realistic. It's still nowhere near as effective as a well planned daily study routine, but as a last resort, definitely worth doing. A key point here is that a night-before cram is *not* an all-nighter; you need to get some sleep. Spend a little time determining a) what you do know; and b) what the possible questions might be. If you don't know anything, and you have absolutely no idea where the exam might be headed, then you at least you have the night before to salvage as much as you can.

Start with those topics that you feel almost certainly will be covered. You don't have unlimited time, so the idea is to only study the content that will give you best possible chance of passing. Cram the most important things first. Get a good night's sleep, wake a little earlier than usual, have a good breakfast, do the last-minute cram in the morning, and then just before you go in the exam room … the last second cram.

Once you are sitting the exam itself, it is important not to panic under any circumstances. You look at the first question, and it's not one of the topics you've covered. *Oh no!* Neither is the second question. *No, no, no! Dear God, NO!* Third question? Zip. *You can picture the disappointment in your mother's eyes. You have let your family down. You are an embarrassment to your generation.* The fourth question is on a familiar topic, but by now you are in too much of a state to answer anything. The only way to proceed is to write something – anything. Don't let all that cramming go to waste. Write whatever you know. Perhaps write about how next time you will prepare more, procrastinate less, and not leave everything to the last night, the last minute and the last second. Enough said.

The myth of 'multitasking'

Technology and innovation have been responsible for so many wonderful new words and expressions. The development of steam-power in the mid-1800s gave us the term "full steam ahead;" now, thanks to Google, we can "Google something." Sometime back in the mid-

DO LESS ... SIMPLIFY

1960s when computers were bigger than the average car, had slowly spinning silver reels, magnetic tape and more buttons and blinking lights than a Boeing 747 – the term "multitasking" was born. It means performing more than one task at the same time; but back in the 1960's the term was specific to computing; and technically ... it was completely wrong.

Computer processors can really only do one thing at a time; but they do those things incredibly fast, giving the *illusion* of multitasking. So they switch back and forth from one task to another, really, really fast. Cognitive research suggests that when it comes to human thought, we're not all that much different to computers, but we're a lot slower. The gist of the research is that the more computers 'switch back and forth', the faster they get, but humans just get more confused. The evidence suggests that our ability to perform multiple tasks simultaneously is quite limited. When attempting to perform multiple tasks, the brain experiences delays as it switches between activities, resulting in reduced efficiency (less attention, less memory and more mistakes).

For students this has huge implications. Any combination of tasks that requires conscious attention (like texting and understanding what the lecturer is saying) will be problematic. It seems that the brain is simply not built to multitask and that nobody is actually good at it, though some are slightly better than others. And if you think you are among the better few, the bad news is that research also suggests that those who *think* they're better at multitasking are usually worse at it. The myth of multitasking persists largely due to the illusion of productivity; it feels busy, but often results in inefficient and poor quality work.

Many years ago, I learned how to juggle. I was certainly not a natural; it took me weeks to get the hang of it. After much practice I could do a basic routine and a few little tricks. My son Chris—who I taught—learned in under an hour. He's *really* good. It's very impressive ... but truly annoying. *[Fun fact: everyone in our family can juggle (except my mother).]*

*#14. You might be able to juggle,
but you can only catch one ball at a time.*

While juggling might seem like multitasking, it's actually a series of single actions, completed one after another. Throw. Throw. Catch. Then throw, catch, throw, catch, and so on ... without dropping a ball. The whole process requires focus and concentration; in fact, that's the reason I wanted to learn. The trick with juggling is realising that you have to first throw the ball in order to catch it. In study-terms 'throwing the ball' means getting rid of any distractions.

As a student, the ability to be able to focus and concentrate is a massive advantage because it contributes to your productivity, how effectively you are able to learn, and ultimately your overall academic success. When you focus, you absorb and retain information better. You work through tasks more efficiently by selecting what to attend to, ignoring distractions, and creating a mental boundary around the chosen task. There must be thousands of school reports with the ubiquitous comment, "needs to pay more attention." The use of the word 'pay' in relation to a cognitive action like 'attention' highlights how focus is treated almost as a currency; something that requires an investment of effort.

That 'investment of effort' is called concentration. The two concepts work together hand-in-hand: you need concentration to be able to focus, and focus requires concentration. If you're working on an assessment, focusing might mean, setting some time aside, finding a place where you can work undisturbed, and gathering all the material you need to complete the task. Concentration is the effort you make to stay engaged for an extended period, avoid distractions, and push through any mental fatigue. It's a skill that (like juggling) you can develop with practice, patience and discipline.

The KISS principle

The KISS principle is based on an acronym that has had quite a few variations ranging from the original "Keep it short and simple" to the more commonly used, "Keep it simple, stupid!" This version is associated with aircraft engineer Kelly Johnson who used it as a fundamental design principle when working with the U.S. Navy in 1960. The idea is that systems work best when they are kept simple. Johnson believed that complex designs increased the likelihood of errors and failures, which could prove critical in a high-stakes environment such as military operations, where reliability is fundamental. The KISS principle eventually spread beyond engineering to many fields as a reminder that simplicity often leads to more successful outcomes.

There is a complexity to modern life that has evolved along with us having greater choice. We have more television stations to choose from, multiple streaming services, thousands of retail outlets, fifty different types of coffee, thirty ways to roast it and a hundred ways to drink it. And if our lives weren't complicated enough, we have social media to keep track of *other* people's lives. Education and the world of study can also be complex.

Courses are often overloaded with content, assessments can be unnecessarily complicated, marking rubrics can be hard to interpret, navigating learning platforms can be overwhelming, and even enrolment itself can be confusing and time-consuming. The key to simplifying life in an educational environment is to be organised; organisation leads to clarity. When you structure your environment, everything becomes much easier to deal with. I often spend more time organising my notes than writing them. It's my way of breaking down a jumble of scattered ideas and thoughts into something that is manageable. It not only creates a clearer mental space, but also gives me a sense of control over the task which ultimately makes it less overwhelming.

If your notes, handouts, and learning resources are disorganised, it makes it harder to find essential information when studying; knowing where to find something means you spend less time looking for it. Make use of binders, dividers, digital folders, or note-taking apps, to keep everything in one place. Highlight or flag essential information in your materials for quick access (I'm a big fan of Post-it notes). The other thing to organise is yourself. Perhaps use a weekly planner to map out study times and prioritise tasks. Having a study plan means you will be more efficient with the time you have. It gives you a clear view of your progress and upcoming tasks, which reduces anxiety and improves focus.

The whole idea behind simplifying things and organising yourself is to free up time. Identifying the 'things that really matter' will depend on the context. If we're looking at the context of study, then the main aim is to stay focused on the essential material and concentrate on core concepts rather than getting lost in minor details. But if we're considering the bigger picture, then keeping things simple and organised, buys you more time to do those things that you really enjoy. Study, at the end of the day, is really just a means to an end.

9. PROCRASTINATION

I'll find a quote for this chapter tomorrow.

Me
Author of this book

Macbeth, Act V, Scene V

"Tomorrow, and tomorrow, and tomorrow ..." So goes the opening line of Macbeth's rumination about futility and the meaninglessness of life. Thankfully, for most students the outlook is not as dire as that; 'tomorrow' is simply another word for 'later' which ultimately translates to 'not now'. The issue in question is procrastination; the act of putting off doing something that needs to be done. Tomorrow is a great place to put everything that we don't want to do today.

Imagine you win $5,000 cash in a raffle and now all you have to do is go and collect it. Would you procrastinate? Probably not. We procrastinate when we're faced with something we don't want to do. Well ... we may want to do it, but just not today (cancel an appointment, ring the bank, start an assessment). Or perhaps you don't want to do it at all (mow the lawn, visit to the dentist, a 3000 word essay). Procrastination is often rooted in psychological and emotional factors that make starting or completing a task feel difficult or unpleasant. We may be worried that we won't do a good enough job, or that the task is too overwhelming, or too boring and tedious. It becomes far easier to distract ourselves with something more enjoyable instead.

That makes sense, because our brains are hard-wired to prioritise immediate rewards over long-term benefits. Throughout history, human survival often hinged on taking advantage of immediate resources, like food and shelter, rather than waiting for a potential future reward. This preference is known as temporal discounting, where we tend to value rewards we can receive right now more highly than those we have to wait for, even if the future reward is larger. Social media, for instance, offers instant enjoyment, while writing an essay may only bring a reward much later.

The tendency to think things will be better in the future is called 'optimism bias'. Tomorrow we'll have more time, be more organised, be better rested, have more energy, and we'll be better equipped to get things done. It makes perfect sense to hand our present-day responsibilities over to our future-self. But as the well known saying goes, "don't put off till tomorrow what you can do today." This is commonly attributed to Benjamin Franklin, however similar sayings have appeared across cultures since biblical times. In a far more contemporary context, Nike has the right idea when they tell us to "Just Do It." It's perhaps the most famous slogan in the world. The implied word at the end of the slogan is "now".

Pressure creates diamonds

There is a general belief amongst students that leaving things to the last minute is a good thing to do. The logic is that it increases pressure and that pressure essentially forces you to complete the task. One of the more common statements I've heard from so many of my students is "I work better under pressure." Really? I mean ... really!? It's the classic "pressure creates diamonds" scenario. We're led to believe that pressure brings out the best in us. So by applying yourself to an assignment at the last possible moment, effectively eliminating any potential safety margin, and subjecting yourself to an enormous amount of self-induced stress, the resulting assessment will actually be better. Better than an assessment that has been carefully and meticulously revised, over a few weeks of calm and well-planned effort? Hmmm. ...

The reality is that while students may think they work well under pressure, planning and pacing your projects always gets the best result. It's definitely a lot less stressful than pulling all-nighters and handing things in at the last possible moment. Delaying tasks until the last minute leaves you less time to address any issues or refine and revise work. The sense of urgency creates a cycle of heightened anxiety, where each instance of procrastination reinforces the feeling of being overwhelmed.

So, the pressure that creates diamonds can also crush cars. Go to any wrecking yard and you'll see what was once a luxury limousine transformed into a small metal cube the size of a suitcase. The impact of procrastination is more than just not doing something. It can sometimes lead to feelings of self doubt and inadequacy; and impacts on how we feel about ourselves. Does this sound familiar?

> "I need to work on my essay today.
>
> I'll just watch one more episode of <insert favourite show>.
>
> Now I'll get started on my essay.
>
> Hang on; I quickly need to tidy my room ...
>
> ... then reorganise my computer files.
>
> *Now* I'll work on my essay.
>
> But it's getting too late.
>
> There's no point in starting now.

PROCRASTINATION

Oh no. I haven't done anything!
I've wasted the whole day.
I'm seriously going to fail.
I am a complete failure."

So somehow we've moved from not completing a task as planned, to being a failure as a person. Procrastination can seem harmless in the short term, but over time, there can be significant emotional and psychological downsides: feelings of guilt for not having done the work sooner, or disappointment for not meeting your own standards. This can chip away at your self-esteem and create a negative self-image, as not only are you failing to meet everyone's expectations, but by constantly putting things off you start to doubt in your ability to manage responsibilities and achieve goals. Over time, this erodes self-confidence and can lead to a sense of helplessness, where you feel incapable of breaking free from the cycle.

While these concerns are perfectly valid, there are quite a few practical strategies that with a little patience and discipline can help overcome procrastination. Start by breaking tasks into smaller, manageable steps so they feel less overwhelming, and set clear, realistic goals for each study session. You don't have to do everything perfectly or all at once – just start somewhere. Remember, every bit of progress, no matter how small, moves you forward. Once you get a taste of how satisfying it feels to be on top of things, you'll find that beating procrastination is not just possible but empowering.

Smoke and mirrors

Playing music has always been part of my life; I can play the piano pretty well, the drums well enough, and the trumpet, not well at all. I'm certainly not a trained musician and I can't read music, but if you have a good ear, master a few basic chord progressions, and practice a bit, it's not all that hard to sound okay – "smoke and mirrors," as I usually say. It's a wonderful expression that originates from the world of stage magic and illusion, but over time has evolved into a metaphor used to describe any situation where there is a distraction, illusion or deception. Procrastination relies on all three.

One of the key features of procrastination is distraction; the art of not doing what you should be doing. A great skill I have is being able to get very busy doing all sorts of things, *except* what the main task is. During the completion of this book, three rooms were totally remodelled in our house, I landscaped our garden, meticulously organised my filing cabinets, and spring-cleaned even when it wasn't spring. I built things, fixed things, and ticked off countless menial items on my never-ending 'to do' list. However, the most dangerous distractions were the ones that that felt legitimate and worthwhile because they were vaguely connected to the task. So reformatting the contents page (yet again), organising my workspace excessively or researching endlessly, all qualify as *plausible* distractions. This is a distraction that seems productive but is not really aligned with your actual goals or priorities. It's important to stay focussed on the task at hand without getting sidetracked by less important or unrelated projects.

You intend to work on an assessment but instead you go off and start working on something else – that's a distraction. When you wait for a burst of inspiration before you can start – that's an illusion. It's a risky strategy because the inspiration you're waiting for may never arrive. Famous artists, writers, inventors and even sports people have all conveyed the same idea: inspiration is a by-product of having the discipline to do what needs to be done. You need to sit down and get to work first.

#15. It's an illusion that inspiration creates great work, when really, it's almost always the other way around.

But what if you're waiting for the right time to start—the perfect time—that's a deception. There is no perfect time. I spent years waiting for the perfect time to finish this book. When I'm not as busy, when I don't have any classes, when the kids are older; the logic was that once the time was right, I will have "clear head space" to finish the book. My doctoral thesis was no different. What should have taken three years, took six. The first three years were a textbook in procrastination. I spent months researching, finding articles, and making notes. I learned how to use citation management programs; I sourced dozens of textbooks, formatted and reformatted pages, and deliberated over fonts. I kept stalling the inevitable hard work, waiting for an elusive 'block of time' that somehow never appeared. I did everything except start writing.

My solution to getting started was to write in short 'bursts'. I used a small teddy-bear shaped kitchen timer (which I still have), set it to 5 minutes and wrote as much as I possibly could, without stopping or editing myself in any way. The logic here is that it doesn't matter what you write, as long as you're writing something. I would keep doing these 5 minute bursts until I either got "in the zone" and started working, or stopped after about a dozen or so attempts. Either way, I produced plenty of interesting material to work with and possibly kick start some ideas.

In the late 1980s, Francesco Cirillo did exactly what I did using a tomato-shaped kitchen timer. He created the Pomodoro Technique (pomodoro is Italian for tomato) which has become a popular productivity tool worldwide. Cirillo experimented with different time intervals, starting with two minutes and extending them up to one hour settling on 25 minutes as the optimal time for his needs. The exact timing is something that you can vary to suit what works best for you. The beauty of the Pomodoro Technique (or my Teddy Bear Timing) is that you don't need large chunks of uninterrupted time to make it work. It's a lot easier to find 5 minutes in a day, than it is to find 2 hours.

Task decomposition

Procrastination is often closely related to the perceived size or complexity of a task. However, there are some tasks that are so daunting that it's difficult to know where to begin. The bigger and more complex the task, the harder it can be to picture finishing it.

The term task decomposition originated within the field of cognitive psychology to describe breaking down complex tasks into simpler, more manageable parts (a bit like the burst writing). This concept gained traction in the 1950s and 60s as researchers in AI and psychology worked to understand human problem-solving and replicate it in machines. Researchers observed that "chunking" information and breaking down tasks into simpler steps not only helped in memory retention but led to greater task completion. It's no surprise, as the average person's short term memory can only hold seven (plus or minus two) units of information –so between five and nine items. If we don't manage to store it into our long term memory, that information is forgotten.

Whether we call it task decomposition, chunking, micro-tasking, setting subtasks or 'mini-goals', the net effect is still the same. We are aiming to break a big task into smaller, more manageable parts. You can break the task down based on whatever criteria you want. For example a 2000 word essay may be tackled a section at a time: introduction, conclusion, method, results and so on. Alternatively, you may chose to break it up into two lots of 1000 words, which translates to four lots of 500 words. Looking at it that way, the task seems far more manageable.

This technique aligns nicely with the concept of spaced and massed learning, which are two different approaches to how we structure learning over time. Massed learning is where you study a large amount of information or practice a new skill in a single session, usually without any breaks. The problem is that your mind may begin to wander, and rather than studying, you end up just staring at your computer, or leafing through pages without actually taking in what you're reading. By the time you realise that your brain has been in hibernation another hour has elapsed.

Spaced learning (or distributed practice) involves spreading out our learning sessions over a longer period, with intervals of rest or other activities in between. Research shows it leads to better long-term retention of information because by revisiting material periodically, you allow memories to consolidate and strengthen over time. Spacing out learning also allows time for mental recovery, which helps avoid cognitive fatigue and overload. This makes it easier to absorb and integrate new information. The collective message of most of the formal studies is much the same: study less, more times.

Embrace the deadline

This has been a difficult chapter for me to write because when I look at the dates on some of my early drafts for this book, they are close to a decade old! How is it possible for me to have procrastinated for so long? I can tell you exactly how ... I didn't have a deadline. Procrastination and deadlines are intimately linked. It's *because* of the deadline that you procrastinate. Without a deadline you're not actually procrastinating, you're just going really, really slowly or ... hibernating, as it were.

#16. A goal without a deadline is just ... a goal.

Setting a deadline is what transforms a goal into a commitment. The hard part, of course, is making sure you actually *meet* the deadline. Finding ways to shift it may offer temporary relief, but eventually you'll be confronted with another deadline looming yet again. I recall doing an online professional development course through a private provider where you had to submit your final assessment by a certain date. If you wanted to shift the deadline, you could pay a little extra to get an extension. There was no limit on how many times you could do this. I got to the point where I had shifted so many times, that the cost of my procrastination was far greater than the cost of the whole course itself; so hard and fast deadlines are a procrastinator's best friend.

If I'm being honest, the only reason I have quite a few completed plays to my name is because the performance dates were already booked in advance. Theatre is a collaborative medium, so I had actors, producers, directors and the future audience to consider. My nightmare scenario was walking out on stage on opening night and announcing to an audience of family and friends, "I know *you thought* you were coming to see a play tonight, but ..." It was the looming deadline that ultimately forced me to finish the play.

Students are more often than not, juggling multiple deadlines, with two or more assessments or exams sometimes falling on the same date. This is quite a common scenario in school and university settings as the structure of many courses are similar – mid semester assessments, and end of semester exams. So rather than being nicely spread out over the semester, there are sudden mountains of work that can't possibly be completed if left to the last minute. It is very important to re-align the deadlines to make completing everything possible. This essentially entails reframing them for selected assessments to smooth out the workload.

In situations when there are no hard and fast deadlines, the only solution is to create one. Self-imposed deadlines become easier to honour when they're concrete, visible, and have meaningful rewards and accountability. I would regularly write down plans with a chapter by chapter breakdown (that would change every week, of course), and create elaborate spreadsheets and work plans (that would also change every week). The danger is that distracting yourself by creating a vast array of plans becomes a form of procrastination in itself; but at least it's a step in the right direction. I would deliberately tell anyone and everyone about this book as it added to the sense of obligation to complete it.

I could not think of a more appropriate place to acknowledge the emotional and positive contribution of the hundreds of students who reacted so positively when I outlined the concept of this book. Every semester I would talk to my class about "the book I'm writing" and they were always so enthusiastic and encouraging. The sense of accountability was almost tangible – I didn't want to let them down (and hopefully I haven't).

10. THE MAGIC OF 50%

Everything in moderation.

My mother
(xx)

Stephen Hawking got it wrong

I was quite a good student in high school. In fact, I was a *very* good student. In Year 8, when I was 14 years old, the stars aligned, and I simply could do no wrong. In science, I scored 100% for every test, every quiz, and every assessment. At the end of the school term I couldn't wait for the report to come out as I knew there would be some sort of financial bonus courtesy of my father. Academic achievement was always rewarded, so 100/100 would surely be a cash bonanza.

The reports were handwritten with a score out of 100 for each subject, a grade, a brief comment by the teacher, and finally, the principal's signature. My reports usually had quite good grades, and comments like, "excellent effort," and "well done, but less talking in class". So you can imagine the keen anticipation for my science mark to be displayed in all its glory. I could just picture it, 100%, A+, "Outstanding, incredible, perfect;" then from the principal, a single word: "Genius." My father would be elated, and the funds would flow.

The report arrived. As expected, really good marks in all my subjects. And science? The mark was 99.9%, with the comment, "Exceptional work Manny ... but there is no such thing as perfection." I couldn't believe it. This man was a science teacher; of course there is such a thing as perfection. Or is there? Either way, my father was elated, the funds did flow ... and I spent years contemplating whether I was cheated out of my rightful mark of 100 percent.

According to the famous theoretical physicist, Stephen Hawking, nothing is perfect. Perfection simply doesn't exist. No doubt my science teacher would agree. I can see the logic. Through a constant string of genetic mutations (imperfections, I guess) the universe has evolved to where we are now. But isn't that ... well ... perfect? Perhaps the answer lies in how we define perfection.

Perfection is relative and if that is the yardstick you use to measure your achievements, perhaps that standard is unrealistic. When my son, Christopher, was about 9 months old he was sitting on the sand staring out at the ocean. It was an idyllic setting, on a beautiful day. We were both contemplating the horizon, each lost in our own thoughts. The difference was ... I had a camera. So to capture the moment I went *behind* him to take the shot. For some reason, that reverse angle appealed to me. I took quite a few family photos like that. It was a time when we shot on film and actually went in to a shop to have the negatives developed. The staff were always perplexed by my photos that didn't even show the subjects face. By all intents and purposes, in terms of modern portrait photography, my photos were a complete fail. But to me, they were perfect. It just depends on the perspective.

*#17. Perfection is almost impossible to define,
let alone achieve.*

In education, the standards for what is considered excellent or "perfect" work can vary depending on a teacher, a grading rubric, or even a particular field of study. Over time, standards and expectations can change. For instance, what would have been considered a perfectly constructed essay a few decades ago might be outdated and clumsy by today's standard. Perfectionism is a big issue for many students. It's more complex than just wanting to do everything well. The problem is when we don't accept anything less than perfect. Oh, and if my Year 8 science teacher is still around, it's not too late to revise that mark.

Goldilocks got it right

If my father had been instrumental in encouraging me to focus on study, my mother's wisdom helped me *not* focus on it. For her, any achievement was a good achievement. She would often (sometimes quite randomly) deliver pearls of wisdom with such confidence and conviction, that I simply had to take notice. English is not her first language, so the syntax wasn't always perfect; but the sentiment was. The key to this chapter is deconstructing her most common refrain: "Everything in moderation." It's self explanatory, but when it comes to study it refers to knowing how much effort you need to put in to achieve the outcome you desire. No more, and no less; just right.

In the classic children's tale, *Goldilocks and the Three Bears* a young girl stumbles upon a cottage in the forest belonging to three bears. Most people know the story. Goldilocks eats the bears' porridge, sits in their chairs and sleeps in their beds. In each case, she settles for the one that was "just right." For Goldilocks, it's the middle ground that provides satisfaction. In so many aspects of life, there's a 'sweet spot' that is neither too much nor too little but "just right". In Eastern philosophy it is conveyed through a sense of balance, yin and yang. The Greek thinker, Aristotle, called it "the golden mean" which is the idea that virtue lies between excess and deficiency. My mother called it "moderation".

There is wisdom to doing just what's needed without overextending. This "bare minimum" approach can be surprisingly strategic, especially when it frees up energy for other things that matter, like rest, hobbies, or spending time with friends and family. There is of course a caveat to "doing just *what's needed*," with emphasis on the words, "what's needed." Some career paths and graduate programs place a greater value on academic performance, particularly in specialised fields. In these cases, a higher GPA (Grade Point Average) is often required; so in these cases, finding the 'just right' balance can be more difficult to achieve.

The "no pain, no gain" philosophy reflects a fairly universal notion that it takes effort and hard work to achieve something worthwhile. My approach, however, was to minimise the effort; what is the *least* amount of pain, to get the greatest possible gain. When I sat the HSC (Higher School Certificate) at the end of my schooling, students received a mark out of 500 to determine their eligibility to go to university. Competitive courses such as Medicine or Law would require marks well above 450, while a standard Bachelors degree needed about 275.

For most of my school years I had my sights set on becoming a doctor, until my senior years when I discovered that being social was way more fun than being academic. I knew I no longer had the motivation or discipline to get the mark needed for medicine, so opted to aim for a bachelor's degree majoring in psychology. The cut-off mark varied every year depending on demand, so I asked my teachers what score they thought would guarantee me entry into my university of choice. Three hundred was the unanimous answer. I scored 302 ... just right.

When good enough is not good enough

For many students, their grades are the only measure of success; but the grades you get aren't necessarily the most important thing – it's what you learn. The saying "it's not the destination, it's the journey," sums it up well. The following scenario is virtually a word-for-word version of an interaction that has been very common during my career as a teacher.

STUDENT: Excuse me, Dr Aston?
    Could I quickly ask you about my assessment?

ME: Sure. You did really well. It was the top mark.

STUDENT: Oh ... yeah, that's great.
    But I was wondering what the problem was?

ME: I'm not sure I know what you mean ...

STUDENT: I only got 87% ... where did I lose the 13%.

ME: Well, it's not really about losing marks, it's more like you *gained* 87 marks. It's a High Distinction.

STUDENT: But I usually get over 90% so I was just wondering where I could improve.

It's certainly a fair question as there is always room for improvement, but in this instance the subtext reveals an underlying disappointment. Even though it was the highest mark in the class, for this student it was still not good enough. For some students the focus remains on their flaws rather than their achievements. Being open to improvement can be a healthy sign of growth as it means you're willing to adapt, learn, and refine your skills. However, there is a nuanced balance between seeing room for improvement and the risk of veering into overachievement.

Overachievers tend to believe that the only thing that matters is getting the best possible grades. They judge themselves by this standard and they also believe that others judge them in the same way. Failure is simply not part of the process. Those who strive for the top grades when studying will usually also be highly successful in everything else they do. Self worth will be measured by success and achievement – a pattern that has probably been there since childhood.

Pressure to obtain high grades, meet deadlines, or excel in extracurricular activities can create a sense of overwhelming stress particularly when nothing feels "good enough," even when it is. Maintaining a high level of achievement across everything you do takes a great deal of time and effort. It's exhausting. The trick is finding that 'just right' spot where you're motivated by potential, not pressured by it. There is no question that achievement is a good thing. It usually means that you value good work and are committed to doing your best; but if those high standards have been obtained by sacrificing your own health and happiness, then the costs may well outweigh the benefits.

There is no 'solution' to being an overachiever because it's not necessarily a bad thing. However, when the goals are set too high, the biggest risk is dropping out for no other reason than self-recrimination for failing to live up to your own high standards. The truth is, when it comes to study, it really is okay to just be ... okay. Education can be quite forgiving; a pass will usually get you the qualification you are after.

The beauty of half-way

Half way as a concept fascinates me. For a start there was far less written about it than I imagined. A Google search resulted mainly in definitions of the word itself and much discussion about whether it is one word or two. Either way, there is no debate that it is the mid-point between two other points. My fascination, however, surrounds the *implication* of arriving at half-way.

Reaching the half-way point in a task or journey is a significant milestone. It gives you an opportunity to reflect on how far you've come and also gives you the chance to change your approach if needed. By half-way you will have far more perspective than you had when you started. No matter how you look at it, from this point on you are now closer to the end than you are to the start, and that's a very good point to be at.

In education 50% is usually the magic number required to pass as it suggests you have achieved a foundational understanding of the material. You may not have mastered it, but you've grasped enough to move on to more advanced concepts without major gaps. Obviously for some subjects, especially ones where safety or precise knowledge is essential (like medicine or engineering), passing marks may be higher to ensure competence.

Still, in practical terms, 50% is seen as a straightforward midpoint, and over time, it has become an accepted standard to signify a pass, making it easy to compare grades across institutions. Fifty percent is the balance between recognising a level of understanding and accepting that students don't need to know everything perfectly to progress.

#18. If you get 51%, you've worked 1% too hard.

It's not just about the marks – marks are only a number. While 'the number' may offer a quick quantifiable snapshot of your performance on a test or assignment, it doesn't capture the full picture of your intelligence, creativity, or potential. Marks can tell you how well you performed on a specific set of tasks, but they don't necessarily reflect what you truly understand.

I recall saying to my daughter in her first year of university, "If you pass all your units, I'll take you out to a nice fancy dinner." It dawned on me that if she works to the best of her ability, attends classes and hands all her assessments in on time, the end result really doesn't matter. What I should have said is, "Even if you *don't* pass all your units, I'll take you out to a nice fancy dinner."

Learning is about developing skills, gaining knowledge, and building character – qualities that last beyond any report card. Students who focus only on marks may ultimately feel limited or defined by them, leading to stress, anxiety, or a sense of inadequacy if things don't go as planned. The realisation that high marks and good grades aren't always the most important thing can be quite liberating.

So here I am, looking at my degrees which are all nicely framed and hanging on the walls of my office. Not one degree states what mark I received. It's the same for the degrees on the walls of any medical clinic, law firm or professional practice. I don't know if my dentist was the top of her class, or whether she just scraped though – all I know is that she is an exceptionally good dentist; and that's all that matters.

All work and no play

One of the most memorable moments in Stanley Kubrick's 1980 film, *The Shining* is when Wendy Torrance discovers that her husband, Jack, has been typing the same sentence over and over. He has essentially filled hundreds of pages with the same line: "All work and no play makes Jack a dull boy." It's when we realise that Jack, who has been working obsessively on his novel for weeks, has well and truly lost the plot. "All work and no play …" is a line I use often for comic relief, when my wife asks me how my writing is going. The sentence, however, has entered popular culture highlighting the dangers of obsessive work leading to burnout.

The term "burnout" was first introduced by psychologist Herbert Freudenberger in the early 1970s. He used it to compare the physical and emotional exhaustion he observed in healthcare professionals, with a candle or a "burned-out" match. It's a particularly accurate comparison within an academic context as students who are struggling will often report feeling physically, emotionally, and mentally exhausted. Academic burnout has become more prevalent as educational demands and pressures have intensified, with many students reporting a loss of motivation, decreased productivity, and a general sense of disengagement from their studies.

During my first year of university, I was keen to prove to myself that I was as talented a student as some of my school reports suggested. I survived the first year with acceptable grades in all my units, and the battle scars from sleep deprivation associated with numerous all-night cramming sessions. By my second year the university environment wasn't so new anymore. I started to feel tired all the time, and even when I did try and get enough sleep, it was rare to sleep well. Headaches became a regular thing, as did frequent bouts of head colds and chest infections. You push a little harder, stretch your days a little longer, believing that more effort must mean better results. But eventually, the returns diminish, and what once felt like progress begins to feel like pressure. It was hard to concentrate, my grades started dropping, and after 13 years of formal education and one year of university, I was exhausted.

For me the solution was to take an extended break. I travelled, worked full time, regained my energy, and after a few years resumed my studies with far greater motivation than ever before. There are so many strategies to combat stress and burnout that it would fill a whole new book. The realm of mindfulness and relaxation offers a great deal of benefits but personally, I found it very difficult to summon a sense of calm amidst the academic chaos.

There are now a myriad of apps targeted at students that focus on mindfulness and wellbeing and all are highly recommended. One technique I found particularly useful, and something I still do to this day, is journaling. I started keeping a journal during my travels initially to simply recall the places I'd been to, but this soon became a way of processing emotions and thoughts. I found that writing things down gave me greater clarity and perspective in whatever task I was engaged in.

Avoiding burnout is about finding a balance between extremes; balancing study with rest and leisure, ensuring that you don't sacrifice your well-being for academic achievement. In the end, moderation is not about doing less; it's about doing what matters most. Let your studies be a *part* of your life, not your *whole* life.

11. THE ART OF FAILING

> Aston's writing is fragmented, aimless, and cumbersome.
>
> *Bob Evans*
> *Drama critic, Sydney Morning Herald*

Self-consciously rusticated

One of my favourite artists is Marcel Duchamp. He was part of the Dada art movement which espoused "anti-art" principles designed to challenge the social norms of society. This is the man who, early last century, presented the art world with the front fork of a bicycle (with wheel still attached) mounted upside-down on a wooden stool. But Dadaist antics aside, Duchamp was an excellent artist. One of his best known works (and the one I like the most), *Nude Descending a Staircase (No. 2)*, had a very dubious start. The art world certainly didn't react kindly to it at all.

The painting features overlapping geometric shapes, rendered in a tawny beige, that are meant to depict a woman's movement down a set of steps. Considering it was painted in 1912, Duchamp's work is quite futuristic. It was very different to the more traditional depictions of the female form, and the general public and critics alike struggled to relate. One famous review in the New York Times called it "an explosion in a shingle factory." Despite its initial reception, the painting is now recognised as a key work of early 20th-century modern art.

Failure within the world of arts and literature is often very public, very personal and sometimes very painful. I can still quote lines word for word from a devastating review of one of my plays, *Clay Soldiers*. "Mostly it is a doggedly descriptive (not dramatic) piece which is decidedly weak on structure," springs to mind instantly. My whole play according to the reviewer was "self-consciously rusticated," and my writing was "fragmented, aimless, and cumbersome." He even criticised the theatre for allowing the play to go on! When I first saw the review, I wanted to run around our street with a pair of scissors, and cut the offending article out of all the newspapers that had been delivered that morning. This wasn't just a bad review … it was a devastatingly bad review, and it had a direct impact on the ticket sales for our season of the play.

Ironically, it was the *only* bad review for that play, and *Clay Solders* had quite a few successful seasons elsewhere. I realised that criticism was a necessary part of the theatre landscape. I just had to learn to deal with it, good or bad. Whether something is a failure or not depends on your perspective. Still, there is no way to sugar-coat it, the experience was definitely not a happy event, and it took quite some time to regain my confidence. While failure in the world of art and literature can be a public affair, it's nowhere near as starkly delivered as in the world of education. A student's result is bluntly presented as a mark out of 100. It's clear, it's definitive and quite often it's brutal. It's hard not to take it personally.

*#19. Failure is never fun;
it's how you bounce back from it that matters.*

My youngest daughter, Emily, was in her first year of university and as it happened, she enrolled in a psychology unit that I used to teach. She was nervous and overwhelmed at the prospect of her first essay at a tertiary level. I did what any father would do. Without actually writing the essay for her, I read over it, corrected a few things here and there, and assured her that, "you probably won't get a High Distinction, but possibly a Credit and definitely a Pass." I should know; as a lecturer, I've marked hundreds of essays exactly like this. Relieved child; hero Dad.

My hero status was maintained until the results were released. A tearful Emily informed me that she had failed. She was fine a few hours later ... she just got on with the job, and without any help from me, still passed the unit. She went on to get quite a few High Distinctions (again, without any help from me). The funny part of this little story is that *I'm* still annoyed about the incident to this day. And that made me think about the notion of how we deal with failure ... and what to do if we decide that study is ultimately not what we want.

Oh, and just in case the person who marked my daughter's Psychology 1100 essay is reading this ... there is no way that essay should have failed. I'm still pretty salty about it. See ... it's hard not to take it personally.

What a cactus and trampoline have in common

Failure. Failing. Fail. The word itself just sounds bad. So much so that some educators have removed it from the educational space preferring the (in my opinion) equally disheartening "not competent." The concept of success and failure is interesting. Are they entities within themselves, or are they relative? As I see it, failure and success are just points along the continuum of achievement, and they are entirely relative. So, failure only exists if you call it a failure. It could just as easily be "not success yet." To borrow from Albert Einstein, "Failure is success in progress."

Dealing with failure as a student can be tough, especially since the educational environment usually places such a strong focus on achievement. But failure can actually be an opportunity for growth, and be part of the learning process. When dealing with any kind of failure, resilience is a key attribute. There has been a lot written about it, particularly within the field of positive psychology. We tend to equate it with "overcoming the odds," being "stress-resistant" and "adaptable." As I see it, the concept of resilience relies on two distinct approaches which are best exemplified by a trampoline and a cactus.

My 'trampoline theory' refers to a person's ability to 'bounce back' from a previously adverse situation. It is characterised by our response to a life event or circumstance; it's not about avoiding failure but about learning to pick yourself up and keep moving forward. If you are able to reframe a difficult experience as an opportunity for growth, it can contribute to a sense of empowerment.

Resilience is also like a cactus which thrives in conditions where many other things might struggle or fail. This type of resilience is based on a personal attribute, rather than a situation. The cactus has evolved to survive in the harsh environment of a desert; it doesn't depend on constant rain, it conserves water, and it grows strong spines for protection. Resilient people don't need perfect conditions to move forward. They find ways to adapt, conserve their mental and emotional resources, and protect their well-being against external stressors.

In education, resilience plays a crucial role. Students who are resilient can handle the ups and downs of academic life – from disappointing grades to difficult subjects. It is a trait that can be nurtured through small, everyday decisions, like setting realistic goals, learning to reframe failures, and embracing challenges instead of avoiding them. When you recognise that setbacks are not final verdicts on your ability but simply part of the journey, you're more likely to learn from the experience and adapt effectively to any change and uncertainty.

It took me 6 years to get my first degree. I was a full-time student, and then a part-time student, then I took a break and finally graduated in the late 1980s. For close to a decade, study wasn't even on the radar, but by the mid 1990's I was teaching in tertiary education and had started thinking about post-graduate studies. I was very keen on a Master of Creative Arts degree that had come to my attention. This would be the perfect bridge between my creative activities and academic theories that would help me develop as a teacher. Certain I would be accepted, I applied (with very little preparation, mind you) and was rejected without even an interview.

What?! Didn't the university realise the calibre of candidate I was? How on earth could I have been rejected? I still recall the range of emotions quite vividly; I was disappointed; angry at myself and the university. Eventually, I regrouped and spent the next year doing a little more research on the degree and exactly what it takes to get into the course. The failure had galvanised my approach and strengthened my determination. I was able to reflect on what I did wrong, and focus on what I should improve. I applied again the following year with a far more compelling application, and was accepted. Little did I know it, but for me, this was the start of 15 years of uninterrupted postgraduate study.

Nothing is impossible ... almost

There was a time in history when the concept of a person flying was impossible until the Wright brothers proved that wrong. Mount Everest was deemed unscalable, the deepest parts of the ocean unexplorable and space travel was incomprehensible; of course, humans have achieved all this and more. Medicine, science and technology have conquered enough 'impossibilities' to fill another book.

There are thousands of motivational quotes, all encouraging us to tackle the seemingly impossible and keep going even in the face of sometimes unsurmountable odds ("when the going gets tough; the tough get going"). Almost every success story will have the obligatory passage of inspirational text describing the odds against which our super-human individual has triumphed. Yet there must be just as many unwritten texts where people—very good people—have paid a heavy price for not quitting.

Robert Falcon Scott was a British explorer who led the ill-fated Terra Nova Expedition to the South Pole in 1912. The weather was brutal and his team was ill-prepared, exhausted and malnourished; yet they pushed on. Tragically, Scott and his men perished on their return trip. His journey, even though it ultimately ended in tragedy, is generally seen as a powerful symbol of human resilience, perseverance and sacrifice. In Scott's case there was a 'greater good' at stake – national pride, the spirit of exploration and quite possibly some personal ambition. The stakes aren't quite as high when it comes to education, however many students react exactly as if they were. They press on, even in the face of enormous difficulty. Stepping away from a goal can be a difficult thing to do, but it's often psychologically healthier than persisting in pursuit of something unattainable.

As a lecturer I've taught many students over the years. Most of the time I could tell how they would go in their course after the first lecture, but one of the great joys of the profession is being proved totally wrong.

One student I remember in particular – they had their hearts set on getting accepted in a degree course that I honestly thought was impossible for them. The student had a non-academic and very challenging family background, struggled in school and based on the first few assessments was struggling in my class as well.

We spent quite a bit of time before and after class, doing our best to make up for 12 years of neglected schooling, but assignments were handed in late, they were full of typographical and grammatical errors, and it was a line-ball call as to whether they would even pass my unit. But this student was so keen and so determined at getting in to their university of choice, I didn't want to be the one to stand in the way – so they passed ... just. The reason I remember this student is because only recently they contacted me after about 15 years. Not only did they graduate from their chosen university, but they are now well established in their field. It was a simple note of thanks, but as a teacher it was one of the best notes I have ever received.

So which is it: "nothing is impossible", or "give up if you have to." I've genuinely struggled to find an answer because they are two equally valid points of view. I asked my son (who won a formal logic prize at university) about his thoughts on my 'nothing is impossible' dilemma. His response via text message was, "Hmmm, let me have a think ... my initial thought is that nothing is impossible, but some things just have a microscopically small chance of happening." I like that response. It's an excellent way to look at it.

Turn on, tune in, drop out

I suspect the iconic counter-culture anthem of "Turn on, tune in, drop out," popularised by psychologist Timothy Leary in the 1960's has something to do with the stereotyped image of a university 'drop-out'. Students at the time questioned the relevance of traditional education; dropping out was seen as both a social statement and a form of rebellion against the conventional educational journey. Today, the term "university drop-out" generally refers to someone who enrols in a university course or program but does not complete it. It carries far less stigma than in the past, however there is still an underlying perception that dropping out is equivalent to failure.

Not everyone who enrols in a course of study will finish. The percentage of students who leave a program of study before completing it is called the attrition rate (or more bluntly, the drop-out rate). It's safe to say that educational institutions want to keep this rate as low as possible. In Australia, the average attrition rate is around 15-20% within the first year. European countries with excellent support systems, such as Germany and

Finland, generally have lower attrition rates, while in countries like Japan, the rates are lower still.

Obviously there are different educational structures and reporting practices, so it's difficult to generalise. In the United States about 20-30% of students leave in their first year. For postgraduate students the drop-out rate is also high, possibly because of a more challenging workload, work commitments, and perhaps because students know they already have a bachelor's degree in their pocket.

The important point to take away from all the statistics is that leaving a program is not uncommon and educational journeys don't always have to follow a set path to be valuable. Degrees and higher qualifications are not always mandated for every career. Success can be achieved in many different ways, and traditional education paths aren't the only way to achieve your goals. It's possibly one of the reasons most universities and colleges give students a few weeks to settle in and see if they are suited to the course. The end of that 'grace period' is called the census date, and it's one that should be on the mind of most tertiary students. Withdrawing from a course before census, usually incurs no academic penalty or financial cost.

The reasons why students may want to stop studying are as varied as the reasons they started studying in the first place. In some cases it's the financial strain of tuition fees and student loans coupled with working part-time jobs (and sometimes full-time jobs), to cover both education and living expenses. In other cases your progress doesn't match the effort no matter how much time and energy you invest. It often comes down to weighing costs and benefits, acknowledging limits, and understanding your goals.

If you've tried everything to make it work and are still hitting walls, it could be a signal that it's time to shift focus. Taking a break can recharge you and help you come back with a clearer sense of purpose, or guide you toward something new that's a better fit. Dropping out or deferring is not quitting; it's simply 'pausing' your study for an indefinite period. You can always return to formal education later in life when you're more prepared, or when circumstances change. Most of my degrees were completed later in life.

There is a very important caveat here, however. You must consider carefully why stopping something is the best alternative. A really terrific piece of advice that I received from my father is: never make any big decisions at a low point. So if you decide to drop out of university because one essay is proving to be more difficult than expected, the best course of action would be to at least complete the essay (to whatever standard you can) and *then* determine whether study is still the right thing for you or not.

I have 'dropped out' of quite a few courses: a diploma course, a Master of Professional Psychology, a second PhD. Some I dropped out of before I even started (Bachelor of Law - what was I thinking); a Bachelor of Archaeology was put on ice thanks to the pandemic, and a recent Graduate Diploma in Neuroscience was shelved two days before the census date because "life just got in the way." Dropping out is not a failure but a strategic choice. It's about recognising when a path isn't right for you at that time. Let's face it, you can always try again later.

The Concorde Fallacy

On the 17th of June in 1972, the supersonic Concorde flew into Sydney for the first time ... and I missed it. I was 11 years old, and extremely disappointed. I recall there had been quite a lot of hype about this event, and I was well and truly invested. The Concorde could cruise at twice the speed of sound. It flew so high that passengers could actually see the curvature of the Earth. I became an instant aeronautical expert reading every article or book that had the word 'flight' in it.

My parents, bless their hearts, bought me an Airfix model of the Concorde, and I must confess, that did go a long way to cheering me up. Well, I was cheerful until I completely botched up the model (as I did with most of the Airfix models I attempted). The real aircraft was unbelievably cool with its distinctive pointy nose and jet-fighter profile, but for a myriad of reasons it became financially unsustainable to keep it in the air. Both the French and the British governments continued to fund it, despite clear indications it would not be profitable. It's a common psychological pitfall in decision-making known as the "Concorde Fallacy" (or 'sunk cost'), where people feel compelled to "see things through" or avoid 'wasting' prior efforts, even if doing so leads to more waste.

#20. *The question isn't whether you should stop studying; it's why should you continue?*

It's often difficult to walk away from a project or commitment when significant time, effort, or money has already been invested; even when rational analysis suggests that stopping is the wiser choice. The old idiom "in for a penny; in for a pound," sums it up well. Now that you've invested so much time and money into something, you really should see it through to the end. However, persisting with an educational program that no longer matches your interests, career goals, or personal values, simply because you've already put in a few years or spent a significant amount on fees and materials is exactly like the Concorde Fallacy.

Letting go doesn't mean failure; it means recognising when a path is no longer the right one and being willing to make a smarter choice going forward. Time and effort are valuable, but so is your long-term satisfaction and well-being. Continuing on a road that no longer leads where you want to go only delays your progress toward a better destination.

A person's goals and priorities can change. Changes in your work or family life, your financial situation, even your interests can have a big impact on whether your studies remain relevant to you. On the tail end of close to 15 years of continuous post-graduate study I had the opportunity to start a second doctorate as a PhD candidate in Psychology. I would be working alongside a friend I had known since I was 10 years old in the exciting new field of cybercrime. Three years into my doctoral studies, I ran out of steam. In my own words at the time, it "just wasn't fun anymore."

Withdrawing from the program was one of the harder academic decisions I have had to make. Not only did I feel like I was letting my friend down, but I felt I was letting myself down. I was already past half-way, had invested so much time and mental effort and had written hundreds of pages. But the end goal had changed; my children were at an age where I wanted to spend more time with them and after four postgraduate degrees back-to-back, I was just simply tired of study.

Study had become a way of life, and it was a difficult thing to stop. My life-long friend completed his PhD with great success and is now a full professor and distinguished academic. The cyber-psychology field has evolved considerably as has the whole cybercrime and cyber-security field. Did I make the right decision? Of course I did. It can only seem wrong in hindsight; at the time I felt the decision was right ... so it was. And let's be honest, there is nothing stopping me from going back and completing the thesis, is there?

12. A ROTTEN FINAL CHAPTER

> My life has no purpose, no direction, no aim, no meaning, and yet I'm happy. I can't figure it out. What am I doing right?
>
> *Charles M Schultz*
> *American cartoonist*

What am I doing right?

Traditionally the final chapter in any non-fiction book should aim to encapsulate the journey, recap the major themes and reinforce any key ideas. The author will look to the future and gently challenge their readers to take action and apply any insights offered to their own lives. This isn't a traditional final chapter. It's a combination of a personal reflection and 'big picture' points that can be applied as much to study as they can to life in general.

It's been such a long journey getting the book to this point so I wanted to get this last chapter right. I decided to ask my children for advice, as all three are or have been students. "How should I finish my book? Answer in any way you want." I wasn't expecting any long considered responses, but was keen to have something for the following morning when I start writing. My son Christopher was the first to respond. After letting me know there would be a brief delay because he is watching something with a friend, he replied (with the caveat that he hadn't actually read the book yet), "Is there any way to put all of what the book is about into practice. Maybe make it meta, and talk about how you used your own manifesto to complete this task."

Gabi was next to respond (no punctuation, as with all her texts): "OMG I'll try but that is a big question and I haven't read the book haha." Her response was quite detailed. "I guess you could end with who you are and why the book is important, or you could do your usually clever dad thing and drop some clues or hints that all make sense in the end. It's hard to know how to end it without reading it a bit to see the vibe." Emily, who has been featured so much in this book, fell asleep, then slept in, and to date has not responded.

I'm not sure if I can do my 'clever dad thing', but the quote that opens this chapter is certainly a good start: "My life has no purpose, no direction, no aim, no meaning, and yet I'm happy. I can't figure it out. What am I doing right?" American cartoonist, Charles M. Schultz would usually channel his own views on life through his *Peanuts* characters, especially Charlie Brown.

But here, it is the man himself who ponders his good fortune at being happy and content despite life's apparent lack of grand purpose or clear direction.

I've never been one to follow a life plan. I haven't had a conventional career; I've never had a 9 to 5 job. As a writer, I've often pondered the meaning of things, only to come to the conclusion that there doesn't always need to be one. One of my favourite personal mottos is, "The universe doesn't owe us an explanation." In revising the final drafts of this book, I asked Chat GPT just to check if the saying was mine. The response really amused me: "No one particularly famous is quoted as saying this - at least not in those precise words."

I've found that there is much joy in simple, unstructured moments. I create things, collect things, restore things, tinker with things, and of course, I write stuff. The 'stuff' in this book is genuinely important to me; I really want it to contribute to making your life as a student more enjoyable. As I mentioned at the start, this is not a 'how to study' book, it's a how to *live with* study book. I've used my own experiences and insights (and a little humour) to reinforce the core messages, provide encouragement, and hopefully leave you with a sense of enthusiasm and inspiration. Of course, it works both ways – the reason this book even exists is because of the enthusiasm and inspiration of the thousands of students I have had the pleasure of teaching over the years.

Formalised curiosity

According to American writer and anthropologist, Zora Neale Hurston, "Research is formalised curiosity. It is poking and prying with a purpose." I love that concept, as curiosity is one of the things that motivate us to learn; it's what drives us to gain knowledge. Children are born with a natural curiosity. They love to explore, ask questions, and make sense of the world around them by investigating everything from how insects crawl around to why the sky changes colour. When we get older, we seem to need a reason to be curious; we learn only what we need to know. As an adult, there is more pressure on us to have the answers rather than the questions.

While curiosity certainly doesn't disappear with age, it sometimes needs to be consciously reignited. That's my excuse for owning thousands of books. Each one has the potential to spark a new interest, or just rekindle and old one. Some are reference works, some are biographies, some have sentimental value, and some are collectible. To me, all of them are interesting. There are books on photography, psychology, motion pictures, biographies, academic texts, humour, and even entire encyclopedias. I have virtually every textbook I used during my years studying psychology. It's a snapshot of my journey; I'm really glad I kept them.

A ROTTEN FINAL CHAPTER

Time Life were well known for their series of books ranging from the great artists (I own that series), human behaviour (own it), photography (own), astronomy (yep), to ancient civilizations (ditto). I have a collection of the Nobel Prize library, every book Oliver Sacks wrote, at least 10 of Edward de Bono's books, the complete works of Samuel Beckett, every *Peanuts* comic strip ever printed, all 24 of the Collins hardcover *Three Investigators* children's book series, and of course, the 20 volume *Oxford English Dictionary*.

Now, I can almost hear you asking … "but have you read them all?" Well … no. Not exactly; but every now and then, I drag a book out and will start to read it. Sometimes I finish the whole book, sometimes I don't. The frightening thing is that even if I read one book a week, I still wouldn't get through them in my lifetime … but there is no harm in trying.

No need to grow up dude

There is a wonderful cartoon by Australian artist, Rod Clement that shows an awestruck kid staring at a long haired drummer. The kid says, "I want to be a drummer when I grow up …". To which the drummer replies, "No need to grow up dude …" A bit of detective work suggests my Dad most likely cut it out of a business magazine around 2012 or so. He was always bemused by me taking up drumming as a 20 year old.

The cartoon reflects something I've often said to my own children many times, "Don't grow up too quickly because you'll be an adult for a long time."

I've spent the better part of five decades 'not growing up'. I own a pinball machine, a tabletop arcade game, a host of magic tricks (that somehow never work for me), lots of puzzles and I build Lego sets (having completely given up on Airfix kits). Fun is the operative word here. Fun is the joy we find in activities that give us energy, spark curiosity, or make us laugh and feel happy. It can come from pursuing hobbies, learning something new, playing games, or even study. It's a stretch, I know, to imply that study can also be fun … but it certainly shouldn't be torture.

In school I was pretty decent at maths, but at university I found statistics difficult. The challenge for me was making it interesting. How on earth could I possibly make statistics 'fun'? Well, I convinced myself it was a bit like learning this secret language which would help me understand the world of psychology in a whole new way. It became a personal challenge to understand the concepts. I recall sitting at our kitchen table clutching my trusty Casio fx-100AU Scientific Calculator, surrounded by a sea of graphs and charts and aborted calculations. Bleary-eyed, tired and "completely over it," I kept reminding myself that "They don't hand out degrees for free," (another mantra I've recited to many students). I knew the hard work would be worth it in the end so I may as well at least take some pleasure in the process.

Finding enjoyment in studying often comes down to shifting your perspective and creating an environment where learning feels rewarding. This becomes a lot easier if you are studying something you are really keen on or have a passion for. As a 17 year old, I mentioned to my dad that psychology seemed like an interesting field. Even though he had no interest at all in the topic, within a week he enrolled us in a community college style evening course. In one of our classes the instructor played a 1961 recording of a talk given by American psychologist, Dr. Murray Banks titled *Just in Case You Think You're Normal*. Without sounding too dramatic, it changed the way I looked at the world, and sparked a lifelong interest in psychology.

Banks was as much a comedian as he was a psychologist. His style was fun and engaging. He spoke about well-being, stress management, and the power of positive thinking. In many ways he was ahead of his time particularly as he combined humour with deeper reflections on mental health; a novel approach in the 1960s, when mental health was often a stigmatised topic. To me, his insights were inspirational and have undoubtedly made their way into my teaching and even into this book.

My Alien

As I write these words the desk in my office faces a wall. I could have placed it near a window that looks out into a lovely garden, with beautiful trees, and a cubby house I built for my children when they were little. But many years ago I learned that a good view just serves as a distraction. On the wall is a large noticeboard that has been there for around four decades, and over time I have built up a healthy collection of photos, notes, postcards, and assorted artworks produced by my kids. The whole thing resembles a postmodernist collage. Some things get taken down; but a majority just stay there much like a personal time-capsule.

Prominent in the top left hand corner is a picture of Michelangelo's sculpture, Pietà. The image for me summed up the theme of a play I was working on at the time. I wanted to have it in front of me while I was writing. Right next to that is a picture that I remember cutting out from the front cover of our telephone directory (back when we had them). It captured the moment 6 year old Pia Jeffrey first heard sounds after receiving a cochlear implant. It's a snapshot of the absolute wonder of suddenly gaining access to a sense that most of us take for granted.

There is my son Christopher's incomparable artwork he called "Formila Sun Ocean." It's essentially a paper plate with a face with 12 irregularly cut strips of orange

A ROTTEN FINAL CHAPTER

paper are glued to this circumference. We never managed to work out what 'Formila' meant – I don't think even Christopher knows. Then there's Gabi's wonderful limerick.

> There once was a girl called Gabi.
> How likes catching crabs.
> She likes pretty shells,
> But hates the sound of bells,
> And was very fab.
>
> [Editor's note: I think "How" was meant to be "Who"]

This lovely piece of work is dedicated "To Mum and Dad," and fully illustrated, of course. However, it is hard to beat Emily's inspiring poem (complete with crayon picture) titled "My Alien."

> My alien is always happy and always smiling. Her name is Penny. Penny lives on Mars. She has lots of friends. She is sometimes sad and confused but mostly she is happy. She is only eight but she is always happy.
>
> My alien is big and very smooth; she also has long straight arms and skinny ears. She is extremely purple. Penny also has a wide mouth and she has no teeth.

My noticeboard puts the world in perspective for me. It reminds me of the things that really matter. Work is only work, study is only study ... and nothing I can ever write will match the inspired prose of Emily's "My Alien."

Finding your 'place'

"Finding your place" refers to discovering where you feel most comfortable: it's about establishing a sense of belonging and finding a connection with a particular environment. I was (and still am) very much at home in the academic environment. The world of study, even if it was challenging at times, was a place where I felt very comfortable.

I vividly remember attending my first psychology lecture with a big grin on my face, clutching my textbook and lined notepad ready to learn about the mysteries of the human mind. The lecture theatre was quite crowded and looked every bit like those I had seen in countless American movies. Twenty five years later I was teaching the same course, at the same university, in the same classroom (not much had changed). It's still a field that gives me a great deal of enjoyment (as I hope is evident with this book).

In 1967, my father was part of the very first intake of students at the newly opened Macquarie University; I recall playing on the campus grounds as the university was literally being built. It's a beautiful campus with tree-lined pathways surrounded by the greenery typical of the northern suburbs of Sydney. I studied at Macquarie, as did all three of my children. As a teacher there, it felt like a second home.

Being a student means you are part of a larger learning community. Academic traditions, shared spaces, and collective activities such as lectures, seminars, workshops, social and sporting activities, all reinforce a sense of inclusion and belonging. Studying gives you opportunities to form meaningful relationships and connections with peers, teachers, and mentors than can sometimes extend beyond academia. Study fosters an environment where collaboration, recognition, and shared purpose are emphasised; it becomes more than an individual activity. I've seen my daughter Emily, spend an entire evening on FaceTime with her best friend Delara, studying. They both sit and work for hours, often without saying a word to each other.

My wife, who began her career as a window dresser, told me she fondly remembers starting her visual merchandising course at the age of 16, exploring the library, going to the canteen, and experiencing the wonder of a whole new environment outside of school. In her words, she felt she was now "part of a bigger picture." Your 'place' can change over time; it might mean finding a new community, career path, or personal mission that suits your current stage in life. Ultimately, "finding your place" is a personal thing that involves understanding your core values, beliefs, and being comfortable with yourself.

I'm sitting in my office that many decades ago used to be a garage. I've written every play, every essay, and every book, in this room. Over the years, the office has evolved to become an extension of myself. It's my 'place.' I'm surrounded by typewriters, vintage cameras, collectibles of all kinds and, of course … books. Near my pinball machine is an old wooden cabinet with glass panelled doors. My mother bought it for $1.00 when the company she worked for was upgrading to more 'modern' furniture. On the cabinet stands an original Grundig valve radio which still works perfectly; it was brought to Australia by my parents in the 1960s. Next to the radio a photo of my father taken when he received his bachelor's degree.

My father was a remarkable man. My mother is also a remarkable woman (partly for remaining married to my father for 63 years!). Her intelligence is far more practical and intuitive. My father's was far more overt. His knowledge of history was encyclopaedic. He spoke five languages fluently and could read and understand Latin.

My dad was a part-time student. He would come home after work, and then study in the evening and on most weekends. Five years of family time is quite a big sacrifice, and one that many mature aged students make. As a student, he was far more conscientious than I ever was. Studying was a serious affair; perhaps a little too serious. When it came to my own education, he was also very enthusiastic; again, perhaps a little too enthusiastic. However, I credit my father as the inspiration and motivation for the bulk of my academic achievements. But, at the end of the day, when it came to his (and my) education, my dad definitely could have been a little more 'rotten'. If he were still around to read this, I honestly think he'd agree.

ACKNOWLEDGEMENTS

A lot of people have already been mentioned in this book, my mother, my father, my wife and my three beautiful children. It goes without saying that I owe all of them my heartfelt thanks. My wife Leanne has the distinction of having read almost every piece of creative work I've ever written, and she's always been honest and constructive (I think "brutal" was the word I used).

My son Christopher read his copy of the third draft and made his (as expected) well thought out and constructive notes. My daughter Gabi and fiancé Laurence dutifully read their draft with Laurence being not only the first to return it to me, but also writing more notes than Gabi. While Gabi's notes were generally brief ('LOL', 'funny', 'good' and 'I like this'), her verbal assessment genuinely meant a lot: "I'll be real with you Dad, I don't normally like non-fiction, but I really enjoyed your book ... and not just because you're my Dad."

Emily's educational journey was featured quite consistently in the book. Pretty much like all her essays and assessments, she gave me everything in the last minute, but the quality was exceptional. It was her insight that ultimately prevailed when considering the order of the chapters.

ACKNOWLEDGEMENTS

To all the students I've taught over the past few decades (and to those who may possibly remember some of the anecdotes contained in this book), I really hope you enjoy reading it.

My colleague and friend Jason Gemenis, has not only been with this project from the start, but is responsible for the inspired front and back cover design. Many thanks, my friend.

Big hugs to my friends and esteemed colleagues; particularly Abbey, Poppy and the team who were there while I was at TFI.

Thanks also to Shen, YY, Chahat and the staff of Inlakesh café where I spend most afternoons writing and drinking my usual "espresso, one sugar".

There are also a legion of wonderful people who have followed the progress of this book. To those who have tactfully asked "Have you finished the book yet?" I'm so pleased to be able to finally answer "Yes."

REFERENCES

1. A ROTTEN CHAPTER 1

4   Shultz, C., M. (1970). *You're a brave man, Charlie Brown.* Fawcett Publications (Coronet Books).

6   American College Health Association. (2019). *National College Health Assessment II: Reference group executive summary Spring 2019.* https://www.acha.org/documents/ncha/ NCHA-III_Spring_2019_Reference_Group_ Executive_Summary.pdf

6   American College Health Association. (2020). *National College Health Assessment III: Reference group executive summary Spring 2020.* https://www.acha.org/documents /ncha/NCHA-III_Spring_2020_Reference_Group_ Executive_Summary.pdf

6   Headspace. (2017). *National tertiary student wellbeing survey 2016.* headspace – National Youth Mental Health Foundation. https://headspace.org.au/assets/Uploads/headspace-NUS-Wellbeing-Survey-2016.pdf

10   American Psychological Association. (2020). *Publication manual of the American Psychological Association (7th ed.).* American Psychological Association.

2. WHAT STRESS ISN'T

13   Cannon, W. B. (1932). *The wisdom of the body.* W.W. Norton & Company

13   Selye, H. (1956). *The stress of life.* McGraw-Hill.

REFERENCES

15   Roberts F. (1950). Stress and the General Adaptation Syndrome. *British Medical Journal.* July 8;104–105.

20   Rickwood, D., Telford, N., O'Sullivan, S., Crisp, D., & Magyar, R. (2017). *National Union of Students National Tertiary Student Wellbeing Survey* 2016. Headspace. https://headspace.org.au/assets/ Uploads/ headspace-NUS-Publication-Digital.pdf

20   American College Health Association. (2020). op. cit

20   Student Minds. (2021). *University mental health charter.* https://www.studentminds.org.uk/charter.html

3. PSYCHOBABBLE

37   James, W. (1902). *The varieties of religious experience: A study in human nature.* Longmans, Green, and Co. https://www.gutenberg.org/ebooks/621

37   Jung, C. G. (1923). *Psychological types* (H. G. Baynes, Trans.). Harcourt, Brace and Company. (Original work published 1921)

37   Maslow, A. H. (1943). A theory of human motivation. *Psychological Review, 50*(4), 370–396. https://doi.org/10.1037/h0054346

37   Peale, N. V. (1952). *The power of positive thinking.* Prentice-Hall, Inc.

40   Schlarb, A., Friedrich, A., & Claßen, M. (2017). Sleep problems in university students; an intervention. *Neuropsychiatric Disease and Treatment.* Vol. Volume 13 (pp. 1989–2001). Informa UK Limited. https://doi.org/10.2147/ndt.s142067

40 Lund, H. G., Reider, B. D., Whiting, A. B., & Prichard, J. R. (2010). Sleep Patterns and Predictors of Disturbed Sleep in a Large Population of College Students. *Journal of Adolescent Health*. Vol. 46, Issue 2, pp. 124–132. Elsevier BV. https://doi.org/10.1016/j.jadohealth.2009.06.016

40 Hershner, S., & Chervin, R. (2014). Causes and consequences of sleepiness among college students. *Nature and Science of Sleep* (p. 73). Informa UK Limited. https://doi.org/10.2147/nss.s62907

40 Keating, X. D., Guan, J., Piñero, J. C., & Bridges, D. M. (2005). A Meta-Analysis of College Students' Physical Activity Behaviors. *Journal of American College Health* Vol. 54, Issue 2, pp. 116–126. Informa UK Limited. https://doi.org/10.3200/jach.54.2.116-126

40 Australian Government Department of Health and Ageing, National Heart Foundation of Australia, & Cancer Council Australia. (2010). *The National Secondary Students' Diet and Activity (NaSSDA) survey: 2009–10: Key findings*. Commonwealth of Australia. https://www.health.gov.au/resources/publications/nassda-survey-2009-10-key-findings

4. THE EDUCATION SYSTEM

55 Robinson, K. (2009). *The Element: How Finding Your Passion Changes Everything*. Viking Penguin.

REFERENCES

5. KNOWLEDGE & LEARNING

60 Kruger, J., & Dunning, D. (1999). Unskilled and unaware of it: How difficulties in recognizing one's own incompetence lead to inflated self-assessments. *Journal of Personality and Social Psychology, 77*(6), 1121–1134. https://doi.org/10.1037/0022-3514.77.6.1121

61 Hoffer, E. (1963). *The ordeal of change.* Harper & Row, p. 34

65 Todes, D. P. (2014). *Ivan Pavlov: A Russian life in science.* Oxford University Press

66 Bandura, A., Ross, D., & Ross, S. A. (1961). Transmission of aggression through imitation of aggressive models. *Journal of Abnormal and Social Psychology, 63*(3), 575–582. https://doi.org/10.1037/h0045925

67 Collins, A., Brown, J. S., & Newman, S. E. (1991). Cognitive apprenticeship: Making thinking visible. *American Educator, 15*(3), 6–11.

69 Deci, E. L., & Ryan, R. M. (1985). Intrinsic motivation and self-determination in human behavior. *Springer Science & Business Media.* https://doi.org/10.1007/978-1-4899-2271-7

70 Akram, I., Ijaz, M., & Ikhram, I. (2017). Role of interest in the learning process. *Educational Psychology Journal, 35*(2), 120–134. Retrieved from https://files.eric.ed.gov

70 Herpratiwi, & Tohir, S. (2023). The influence of learning interest and discipline on learning motivation. *International Journal of Education in Mathematics, Science, and Technology (IJEMST)*. Retrieved from https://files.eric.ed.gov

6. INFORMATION OVERLOAD

73 Dickson, A (2018) "Inside the OED: can the world's biggest dictionary survive the internet?" *The Guardian*, 23 February 2018

73 Simpson, J. A. & Weiner, E.S.C. (eds.) (1989) *The Oxford English Dictionary*. 2nd ed. Oxford: Oxford University Press.

74 Kasner, E., & Newman, J. (1940). *Mathematics and the imagination*. Simon and Schuster.

74 Google, v.². (2023). In *Oxford English Dictionary*. Oxford University Press. https://doi.org/10.1093/oed/5409369308

76 Hahn, H., & Stout, R. (1993). *The Internet yellow pages*. Osborne McGraw-Hill

77 World Book Encyclopedia. (1917). *Preface. In The world book: Organized knowledge in story and picture* (Vol. I). Hanson-Roach-Fowler Company.

80 Gross, B. (1964). *The managing of organizations: The administrative struggle* (Vols. 1-2). Free Press.

80 Toffler, A. (1970). *Future shock*. Random House.

81 Hertwig, R., & Engel, C. (Eds.). (2016). *Deliberate ignorance: Choosing not to know*. MIT Press.

REFERENCES

7. GETTING STARTED

93 Hershner, S., & Chervin, R. (2014). Causes and consequences of sleepiness among college students. In *Nature and Science of Sleep* (p. 73). Informa UK Limited. https://doi.org/10.2147/nss.s62907

93 Johnson, R. (2024). Sleep deprivation in students: Impact on academic performance and well-being. *NeuroLaunch*. Retrieved from https://neurolaunch.com/sleep-deprivation-in-students/

97 Hill, N. (1937). *Think And Grow Rich*. The Ralston Society

97 Byrne, R. (2006). *The Secret*. Atria Books

97 Merton, R. K. (1948). The self-fulfilling prophecy. *The Antioch Review, 8*(2), 193–210. https://doi.org/10.2307/4609267

8. DO LESS ... SIMPLIFY

102 Biederman, M. (2019). *Scan artist: How Evelyn Wood conquered America*. Chicago Review Press.

107 Uncapher, M. R., & Wagner, A. D. (2018). Minds and brains of media multitaskers: Current findings and future directions. *Proceedings of the National Academy of Sciences*. Vol. 115, Issue 40, pp. 9889–9896. https://doi.org/10.1073/pnas.1611612115

107 Broeker, L., Liepelt, R., Poljac, E., Künzell, S., Ewolds, H., de Oliveira, R. F., & Raab, M. (2017). Multitasking as a choice: a perspective. *Psychological Research*. Vol. 82, Issue 1, pp. 12–23. https://doi.org/10.1007/s00426-017-0938-7

108 Janssen, C. P., Gould, S. J. J., Li, S. Y. W., Brumby, D. P., & Cox, A. L. (2015). Integrating knowledge of multitasking and interruptions across different perspectives and research methods. *International Journal of Human-Computer Studies, 79*, 1–5. https://doi.org/10.1016/j.ijhcs.2015.03.002

108 Kirschner, P. A., & de Bruyckere, P. (2017). The myths of the digital native and the multitasker. *Teaching and Teacher Education, 67*, 135–142. https://doi.org/10.1016/j.tate.2017.06.001

9. PROCRASTINATION

121 Miller, G. A. (1956). The magical number seven, plus or minus two: Some limits on our capacity for processing information. *Psychological Review, 63*(2), 81–97. https://doi.org/10.1037/h0043158

121 Baddeley, A. D., & Hitch, G. J. (1974). Working memory. In G. A. Bower (Ed.), *The psychology of learning and motivation* (Vol. 8, pp. 47–89). Academic Press. https://doi.org/10.1016/S0079-7421(08)60452-1

123 Cepeda, N. J., Pashler, H., Vul, E., Wixted, J. T., & Rohrer, D. (2006). Distributed practice in verbal recall tasks: A review and quantitative synthesis. *Psychological Bulletin, 132*(3), 354–380. https://doi.org/10.1037/0033-2909.132.3.354

123 Roediger, H. L., & Butler, A. C. (2011). The critical role of retrieval practice in long-term retention. *Trends in Cognitive Sciences, 15*(1), 20-27. https://doi.org/10.1016/j.tics.2010.09.003

123 Ebbinghaus, H. (1913). *Memory: A contribution to experimental psychology.* (H.A. Ruger & C.E. Bussenius, Trans.). Teachers College, Columbia University. (Original work published 1885)

10. THE MAGIC OF 50%

127 Hawking, S., & Mlodinow, L. (2010). *The grand design.* Bantam Books.

136 Duke University. (2024). *Why perfectionism can lead to poor performance.* Duke Learning and Organization Development. Retrieved from https://sites.duke.edu/lodtraininghub/2024/04/01/why-perfectionism-can-lead-to-poor-performance

136 Freudenberger, H. J. (1974). Staff burnout. *Journal of Social Issues, 30*(1), 159–165. https://doi.org/10.1111/j.1540-4560.1974.tb00706.x

136 du Toit, A., Thomson, R. & Page, A. (2022). A systematic review and meta-analysis of longitudinal studies of the antecedents and consequences of wellbeing among university students. *International Journal of Wellbeing, 12*(2), 163-206. https://doi.org/10.5502/ijw.v12i2.1897

11. THE ART OF FAILING

140 d'Harnoncourt, A., & Hopps, W. (1973). Etant Donnes, reflections on a new work by Marcel Duchamp. *Philadelphia: Philadelphia Museum of Art.* (First published in Museum Bulletin, 1969).

140 Evans, B. (1990, June 25). *This club act needs more work.* Sydney Morning Herald

148 Horrocks, M., Shearman, D., Colbourn, A., & McGlynn, S. (2024). A study of the relationship between student retention and mathematics and statistics support in an Australian university. *International Journal of Mathematical Education in Science and Technology* (pp. 1–20).. https://doi.org/10.1080/0020739x.2024.2422826

149 National Center for Education Statistics. (2023). Undergraduate retention and graduation rates. *U.S. Department of Education.* Retrieved from https://nces.ed.gov/programs/coe/indicator_ctr.asp

12. A ROTTEN FINAL CHAPTER

158 Hurston, Z. N. (1991). *Dust tracks on a road: An autobiography.* Harper Perennial. (Original work published 1942)

161 Banks, M. (1961). *Just in case you think you're normal* [Audio recording]. Murmil & Associates.

THE ROTTEN STUDENT MANIFESTO

#1. It's only stress if you perceive it to be.

#2. The best way to stop a giant snowball forming is not to roll it down the hill in the first place.

#3. The key to changing a negative thought pattern is to recognise that it is in fact, negative.

#4. There are times when there may be no obvious positives; this is when simply 'not being negative' is good enough.

#5. The best way to sound smart is to reference someone smarter.

#6. It's important to remember, the goal of education isn't just academic achievement; it's helping you discover who you are and who you want to become.

#7 The trick to understanding something is knowing exactly how much you need to understand.

#8. Learning is a fundamental human skill that enables us to develop and adapt to a world that is constantly changing.

#9. Your life as a student will be ruled by the quality and quantity of words you use; the dictionary should become your new best friend.

#10. The world has become a chaotic place, and the internet only amplifies the noise. Finding clarity in the chaos is a superpower.

#11. When planning anything, the only thing you can expect is that it will take more time than you expected.

#12. It's the right path until you figure out that it's the wrong one.

#13. The only person who should be reading a textbook word for word, is the person who wrote it.

#14. You might be able to juggle, but you can only catch one ball at a time.

#15. It's an illusion that inspiration creates great work, when really, it's almost always the other way around.

#16. A goal without a deadline is just ... a goal.

#17. Perfection is almost impossible to define, let alone achieve.

#18. If you get 51%, you've worked 1% too hard.

#19. Failure is never fun; it's how you bounce back from it that matters.

#20. The question isn't whether you should stop studying; it's why should you continue?